GW00857392

Hola, Ami

Around Central Amer

Jason Smart

First English edition published in 2018 by Smart Travel Publishing

The moral right of Jason J Smart to be identified as the author of this work had been asserted in accordance with the Copyright, Designs and Patents Act, 1988

Cover design by Ace Graphics

ASIN: 9781520328256
ISBN-13: 978-1985145290
ISBN-10: 1985145294

Smart, Jason J
Hola, Amigo!

ALSO BY JASON SMART

The Red Quest

Flashpacking through Africa

The Balkan Odyssey

Panama City to Rio de Janeiro

Temples, Tuk-tuks & Fried Fish Lips

Bite Size North America

Rapid Fire Europe

Crowds, Colour, Chaos

Meeting the Middle East

From Here to Anywhere

Africa to Asia

An Accidental Tourist

Take Your Wings and Fly

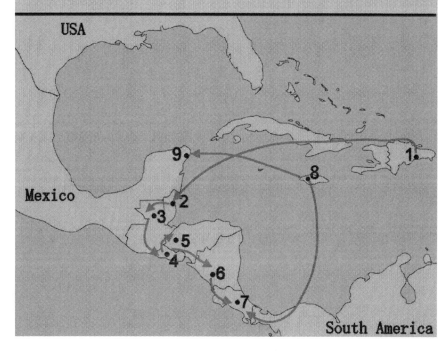

1. Santo Domingo, Dominican Republic
2. Belize City, Belize
3. Flores, Guatemala
4. San Salvador, El Salvador
5. Copan, Honduras
6. Managua, Nicaragua
7. San Jose, Costa Rica
8. Montego Bay, Jamaica
9. Cancun, Mexico

USA

Mexico

South America

Contents:

Jason Smart

Hola, Amigo!
Around Central America and Beyond

SMART TRAVEL PUBLISHING
MANCHESTER

Chapter 1. Santo Domingo, Dominican Republic

FCO Travel advice: There have been a number of incidents in Santo Domingo where foreigners have been mugged at gunpoint during the daytime.

When the United States of America banned me from setting foot inside their glorious nation, I knew that getting to Central America was going to be difficult. From Europe, the cheapest flights to that part of the world connected through places such as Miami or New York but with a five-year travel ban in place (of which I still had four years left to run), I had to find an alternative route to Central America. In the end, my plan was to fly from Manchester to Brussels, stay the night in an airport hotel and then catch a holiday charter flight to Santo Domingo, capital of the Dominican Republic. Not quite Central America, but near enough for my purposes.

So why had America banned me? The answer was simple: the previous year, while living in the Middle East, I had decided, much on impulse, to visit Kish Island, only a short flight from Dubai. And the problem with Kish Island was that it was part of the Islamic Republic of Iran. Nevertheless, the small tropical island welcomed me with smiles and open arms, stamping my passport so that I could remember my fleeting day-only visit. It was a great trip, where I met some of the friendliest people in all my travels, and I returned to Dubai a happy man. Soon after, I received a sting in the tail, courtesy of the United States Homeland Security. They had decreed that anyone who had visited Iran – even Kish Island – would not be allowed in for five years, which was a major pain in the arse. They would not even allow me to transit one of their airports on the way to somewhere else. But there was one positive: in order to get to Central America, I had to go via the Caribbean. Which was no bad deal, I felt.

So, on a rainy day in Northern England, I flew into an equally rainy day in Brussels. That night, sitting alone in an airport hotel as drizzle spattered the window, I looked over my plans for the coming few weeks. Nine countries were on my madcap itinerary, meaning it was going to be busy. I would be flying between colonial-rich Central American capital cities, stopping off at Caribbean coastal towns and traipsing through steamy jungles full of Maya ruins. I was especially looking forward to Costa Rica and Nicaragua, both of which I'd heard good things about. Nicaragua was *the* up-and-coming Central American destination, attracting tourists by the planeload now that it had shaken off its old revolutionary ideals and embraced its volcanoes and lakes instead. Costa Rica was famous for its wildlife and I was looking forward to seeing some of it. Conversely, other places worried me: El Salvador, for instance. The smallest country in Central America was gripped by gang warfare, wasn't it? Would my travel insurance pay out if I was taken hostage or shot? It was the same with Honduras and Guatemala. Both countries were synonymous with murder and drugs cartels, weren't they? But it was too late to worry about any of that now. Instead, I closed the curtains of my tiny room and slept fitfully, as I always did before a major trip.

The next morning I boarded my flight to Santo Domingo, stuffed into the middle aisle with a bunch of Belgian holidaymakers. With a nap here and a movie there, the time passed in a blur of boredom and tedium. When we landed in the Dominican Republic ten hours later, my fellow passengers clapped with glee; overcast Belgium had been replaced with Caribbean sunshine. The first stop of my nine-country extravaganza was about to begin.

2

"The rate is thirty-six peso to the dollar," said the young woman behind a currency exchange counter of Las Américas International Airport. Behind me, my fellow Brussels passengers were clattering past with their hand luggage and hats.

"Thirty-six?" It seemed low.

She nodded, yawning. Like many people in the Dominican Republic, the woman's features were a mixture of ethnicities, a holdover from Spanish colonists having relations with their African slaves. While she waited, I checked an important slip of paper in my wallet. Before any trip, I always made a note of how much one US dollar was worth in all of the foreign currencies I would be using. It told me the official rate was forty-seven Dominican pesos to the dollar, meaning the rate the woman was offering was paltry. However, I needed the cash for the taxi ride and nodded and handed over a hundred-dollar bill.

The woman took it just as another charging horde of passengers came. Armed with iPads, bottles of sun cream and the loudest voices of any nation on Earth, it was a pack of passengers from a flight arriving from New York. *Bloody hell*, I thought. If I delayed getting to immigration any longer, I would be there for hours. As soon as the woman passed me a wad of limp and pathetic pesos, I was off, racing to get ahead of the American crowd. It was a good job, because when I turned a corner I found myself at the back of an already-horrendous queue.

As I shuffled forward, I wondered when air travel had turned into one long process of queuing. Queue to check-in, queue to board the plane, queue for the toilet once aboard: queue, queue, queue. The glory days had ended in the 1970s, I reckoned. Nowadays, air travel was a chore. By the time I was stamped into the Dominican Republic, it was 3.50 p.m. but 8.50 p.m. back in Belgium. I successfully stifled a yawn and braved the throng to find some transport to the city centre.

My taxi driver was a young man with poor English. With my Spanish linguistic skills even poorer, our conversation ground to a halt before we had even left the airport boundary. Instead, the driver switched on the radio, tuning to a channel dedicated to nonstop *bachata* which, to my untrained ears, sounded like Salsa music on steroids. Almost immediately, the driver started bobbing his head in time to the guitars and bongo drums.

The backdrop outside was perfect for the soundtrack: a turquoise Caribbean Sea lapping along a deserted stretch of sand, punctuated by deliciously tropical palms. Palm trees always looked good, I mused. The sway of their fronds, the curve of their trunks and the promise of coconuts made them symbols of the tropics, totems to vacationers from colder climes. The Dominican Republic is famous for its beaches, which is why it is the most popular island in the Caribbean. Almost every arriving passenger at the airport would be passing these beaches on their way to their all-inclusive resorts. Hardly any would venture to the capital, Santo Domingo, which was where I was staying for the next two nights. With the salsa-type rhythms coming from the speakers, we passed a series of unusual but striking sculptures: a reaching green fist; a huge pair of bronze fish, and a reclining yellow mermaid, her tail jauntily raised towards the sky. Even a petrol station wanted to add some Latin flavour: Tropigas was its name, a moniker that could have graced the album cover of any bachata band.

The other side of the road was less flavoursome, made up of auto-repair garages, car wash establishments, cement stores and a café that offered billiards and a disco. Towering above them was a series of tall-columned billboards advertising everything from plasma TVs and mobile phones to the usual suspects specialising in fast food. While I took everything in, I found my fingers tapping away to the infectious rhythms coming from the radio. The driver was doing the same thing on the steering wheel. As we drove along the curving coastal road, he upped the ante by humming along to a trumpet refrain; I nodded in appreciation, making him smile.

As we approached the central part of Santo Domingo, a clump of skyscrapers appeared in the distance. They were the corporate headquarters, the new shopping malls and the shiny apartment blocks of a nation on the up. The Dominican Republic has the largest economy in the Caribbean and these modern developments were evidence of that. Even my hotel had at least ten levels, each one overlooking the ocean. As we parked outside, I saw a minibus pull up behind us. From it spilled the Belgian flight crew who had flown me across the Atlantic. As they collected their luggage, I paid my driver his fare and headed inside, fighting off the urge to simply drop onto the nearest chair to go to sleep. I was so tired that once I was up in my room I did exactly that, though I slept not on a chair but on a bed. An hour later, I forced myself awake and spent the remainder of the evening having something to eat and planning my sightseeing tour for the next day.

3

The next morning I awoke with a start at 6 a.m. The previous night I'd forced myself to stay awake until 9 p.m. before conceding defeat and flopping into bed, immediately falling into deep slumber. Sleeping straight for nine hours was great for my internal battery but, with nothing to do at 6 a.m., I dozed, twisted and turned until I could see some sun creeping from behind the curtains and then got up and looked at my map of Santo Domingo.

There were a few cathedrals to see; I had circled them the previous evening. There were also a few plazas, lots of ruins and a fort. During breakfast, I used the hotel wi-fi and logged onto the British Foreign Office website to read the latest updates. In dry terms, it stated that the Dominican Republic *'suffers from a high crime rate, ranging from opportunistic crime, like bag snatching and pick-pocketing, to violent crime. Don't wear expensive jewellery or carry large amounts of cash or expensive items like smart phones or cameras on the street. If you're attacked or mugged, don't resist.'*

I sighed. The warning had not changed since I'd left the United Kingdom. The sentences made the Dominican Republic sound downright dangerous. But warnings always did: that was their job, and without them, people might end up robbed or murdered. But warnings like this had to be taken in context. Bag snatching happened everywhere in the world, and people stole mobile phones on the nicest streets in the UK. And in over one hundred countries, with warnings about pickpockets in most of them, I had only been pickpocketed once, and that had been while drunk in Prague over a decade previously. Nevertheless, I decided to heed the warnings at face value: I removed some crumpled pesos and then put my wallet in the hotel safe. After stuffing the pesos into a zipped pocket of my trousers, I shoved my camera and phone in too. Just before I stepped out onto the mean streets of Santo Domingo, I paused at one of the hotel desks and asked the woman behind the counter whether it was safe to wander around outside alone.

"Where are you going?" she asked.

"Just to see the fort and the main plazas."

"In that case, you should be fine. If you're staying in the Colonial Zone, during the day it is safe. Just keep to the main streets and don't get your camera out too often. But make sure you are not outside after dark, even in the Colonial Zone. Many bad people are around at night."

I thanked the woman and headed off into a warm and sunny morning in the Dominican Republic. That was one of the good things about the Caribbean and Central America: it was always warm. Sure, there might be a few hurricanes to contend with or the odd tropical downpour, but at least the temperature could always be relied upon.

George Washington Avenue, the coastal road outside my hotel, was busy with the morning rush – taxis, old Mack trucks, modern buses and decrepit minivans made up much of the traffic, thickened by sleepy commuters driving along in their cars. Beyond the road was the sea, a warm wash of blue lined with palm trees and a couple of bulldozers. The only people, apart from those in vehicles, were a foursome of road workers standing with shovels near the bulldozers, and a couple of women walking underneath handheld sunshade parasols. None of them looked like muggers or thieves. Five minutes into my walk, I breathed easily and took a photo of the Caribbean Sea. Quick as a flash, the camera was back in my pocket.

At a roundabout, I came to a towering obelisk. Painted upon the giant spike of granite were images of young women. One was reading a heavy tome, perhaps a Bible. She looked saintly in her flowing robes, with a vast wreath around her head and a Dominican Republic flag draped over her shoulders. Around the other side, a similar-looking woman was playing a woodwind instrument. A third woman was releasing butterflies. They were the Mirabal sisters.

4

In 1935, when the obelisk had been commissioned, the Mirabal sisters were all little girls. While they grew up, the Dominican Republic was under the iron rule of Rafael Leonidas Trujillo, a moustachioed man with a preference for slicking back his mane of thick black hair. Trujillo would come to detest the sisters.

Even as a teenager, Rafael Trujillo was a bad apple, preferring stealing cattle and robbing post offices to studying or working on a farm. Eventually he joined the army, where he managed to leave behind his life of petty crime to become, by all accounts, an excellent soldier, eventually rising to the rank of Commander-in-Chief. In 1930, aged thirty-nine, Trujillo took advantage of a coup and installed himself as president. One of the first things he did was rename the capital after himself. Overnight, Santo Domingo became Trujillo City, and the great man wanted a big obelisk to commemorate this. It was one of his less tyrannical ideas, but one of the most visual. One of his other grand schemes involved organising a huge party to crown his daughter as queen: an event that blew a third of the national budget. Then he started a campaign to get his wife awarded the Nobel Prize for Literature, even though she had never written a book. So when he ordered the obelisk, no one really batted an eyelid.

With the top job in his hands, Trujillo banished all opponents and ordered factories to begin mass production of statues of his likeness, which were then placed everywhere. Then he had a huge sign put up in the middle of the city that said *God and Trujillo*. When one of his sycophants pointed out that people couldn't see it at night, he had some electricians fit lights so it was illuminated. Then he had the sign renamed to say *Trujillo and God*. More lights were added and then the sign was made larger. At the same time, his state-sanctioned newspapers declared how honourable the president was – on the front page of every issue. Things took a bizarre turn when a colonel's position came up in the army and Trujillo gave it to his son, even though he was only four years old.

But Trujillo's oppressive ways had one remarkable effect on the country. After decades of stagnation and poverty, the economy hit full stride under his iron hand. Foreign investment poured in. Instead of siphoning it all into his private accounts, Trujillo built universities, improved the country's infrastructure and paid off the national debt. Many citizens began to enjoy a period of prosperity. But then unsavoury aspects of Trujillo's private life began to emerge. His ridiculous collection of neckties came under scrutiny. Instead of owning just one or two, or even twenty, Trujillo had ten thousand. His unquenchable sexual appetite – a thirst none of his three wives had ever been able to satisfy – became public knowledge. His harem of mistresses and escorts was frowned upon, as was the trick commonly employed by anyone wanting to curry favour with the president. To grease negotiations, ministers often brought young women along as bargaining chips. And under this backdrop, the Mirabal sisters, now adults, preached their sermons about how evil Trujillo was. In response, he threw them in prison. That's why, back then, none of them would have featured on his special obelisk. Unless they were hanging from it dead.

He might have killed them, too, if it hadn't been for America demanding their release. But when they left prison, the sisters carried on where they had left off, telling anyone who would listen that Rafael Trujillo was a crazed dictator who needed to be stopped.

To silence the women once and for all, he ordered their secret execution. In November 1960, as three of the sisters were driving into Trujillo City, a gang of the president's henchmen stopped their car, dragged the women out and clubbed them to death. That done, the attackers stuffed the sisters' bodies back into the vehicle, drove it up to an isolated hillside and pushed it over the edge, reporting their deaths as a terrible accident.

Except no one believed it.

When the truth emerged a few years later, the Mirabal sisters were regarded as martyrs. And that was why Trujillo's obelisk was now covered in paintings of them.

Things came to a dramatic end for Rafael Trujillo in 1961. After thirty-one years in power, his car was ambushed and he was shot dead. Soon after, his cronies were kicked out of the country and Trujillo City reverted to its original name of Santo Domingo.

5

I turned away from the sea road, heading inland. Here I found more people going about their business. Most looked like they were walking to work, but some were sitting outside shops on plastic chairs, protecting their fried snacks or convenience goods from pilfering hands. Some store owners were sloshing water over the cobbles. Everyone looked friendly and peace-loving, which was not that surprising, as the citizens of the Dominican Republic enjoyed one of the highest GDPs in the Americas, comparable to that of people living in Brazil and Costa Rica. Haiti, on the other hand, just next door in geographical terms, was a world away in terms of economic advantages. Its citizens languished with a GDP eight times less, hovering in the lower reaches of the league table between Afghanistan and Sierra Leone.

"Hola, amigo!" a man uttered from the other side of the street, as if to prove how friendly the folk were in Santo Domingo. When I looked his way, he jabbered away in Spanish, pointing at his impressive array of sunglasses. Further along, an old woman said hello for no other reason than we were fellow human beings passing along the same stretch of pavement. Things might have been different if I was walking further north, in the Capotillo district of the city, where almost a hundred-thousand people were crammed into an area less than two square kilometres. If I wished to be a victim of crime, then Capotillo would be the place to be. For the middle class of Santo Domingo, Capotillo was a place to avoid. Aside from the risk of crime, it reminded them of the vast gulf between their lives and the lives of the have-nots.

From somewhere came the sound of a trumpet. It sounded like someone playing behind a high wall I couldn't see over. Then the trumpet stopped and a clarinet replaced it. I rounded a corner and found myself at the entrance to Independence Park. From a shaded position beside a large stone wall, a group of uniformed policemen were rehearsing. While I watched, the trumpeter screeched back into discordant action, much to the amusement of his pals. It sounded like a cat fight. The sax player shook his head and guffawed.

I left them to it, finding that, instead of plants and trees, Independence Park was full of statues and flags, together with a grand building known as the Altar of the Homeland. With its white marble exterior and sweeping white staircase, it could have been the tomb of an ancient river god in Egypt, except it was a mausoleum for the Dominican Republic's three founding fathers who were buried in its crypt. At the entrance stood three huge marble statues of them: Juan Pablo Duarte, Francisco del Rosario Sanchez and Ramon Matias Mella. Collectively they were responsible for kick-starting the Dominican Republic's independence movement against Haiti, who had occupied the whole island at the time.

I stared up at the statues in turn; each man looked suitably stately and solemn in white. When the music started again, this time tuneful and controlled, I left the park to find the main central core of colonial Santo Domingo, supposedly the oldest continuously occupied European settlement in the New World.

6

Santo Domingo's main central square is called Parque Colon. It is bordered on one side by a busy café (which, when I looked, was serving up frothy lattes to a gathering of American tourists), a cigar museum, an amber museum and an empty store guarded by an elderly security guard. He was sitting on a white plastic chair looking utterly bored, not even a mobile phone to keep him entertained. I wasn't bored; I was too busy watching everyone going about their business.

Trinket hawkers were setting up their stalls while blue-shirted tour guides waited to pounce on any passing tourist. A tout from the amber shop was chatting to a couple of policemen who were watching things from a shady spot under a tree. Just along from them were a couple of old geezers on a bench talking animatedly about something so serious that one of them stood up and yelled at the other. The policemen looked over but when the man sat back down they returned to their conversation with the amber-shop employee. It was still not even 10 a.m. I found an empty bench of my own to enjoy the spectacle of a Santo Domingo plaza as it readied for another day of business.

A man with a set of necklaces dangling enticingly over his raised arm walked towards my bench. When he got closer, I realised they were not necklaces but Rosary beads. Tiny metal crosses hung at the end of each chain. The man smiled expectantly, awaiting my decision.

"No, Señor," I said, pulling an apologetic expression. "No para mi, gracias." *Not for me, thanks.* In just two short sentences, I had used up virtually all of my Spanish vocabulary. The man nodded, already walking away, his keen eye noticing a foursome of Westerners approaching from the eastern corner of the square. With his departure, I turned my attention to a small crowd hovering around two gents playing backgammon. Undertaken in contemplative silence, with only the clicking of the counters making any noise, the game looked deadly serious. Suddenly, one of the players snorted and stood up, much like the man on the bench had done earlier. The disgruntled man pointed to his opponent's piece and tutted. Half the crowd were nodding in agreement. Clearly backgammon was no laughing matter in the Dominican Republic.

But not as serious as backgammon is in Russia. In 2008, in a dingy Moscow flat, a man bet his life that he could beat an opponent at a game of backgammon. When he lost, the victor, a 35 year old Muscovite called Sergei Smirnitsky, nodded thoughtfully, walked to kitchen, grabbed a kitchen knife and stabbed him to death. But with a dead body littering his domicile, Smirnitsky had a messy problem; he decided to enlist the help of his next-door neighbour. After knocking on the man's door, Smirnitsky politely asked him to help drag the corpse from his eighth-floor room to the street in order for a proper disposal to be carried out. His neighbour considered this, then slammed and bolted the door before ringing the police.

A couple of pigeons drew my attention. One, clearly the male, had puffed out its chest to impress a female, who was pecking by a statue in the middle of the square. She seemed unimpressed with his display, so he jumped onto a step, flapped his wings and puffed out his chest even more. She glanced his way, but then turned tail and flew off. Her suitor watched her go and then sucked his chest back in and found a perch in a tree above me. More pigeons were frolicking in a nearby puddle. At first I thought they might be drinking from it but, as far as I could tell, they were simply paddling, as if biding their time for something more exciting. And then I realised what it was – a man selling seed. With an audience of Western teenage girls, he poured some seed from a bag until the palms of his hands were covered. Then, like a Biblical miracle man, he raised his arms to shoulder height and waited until two pigeons landed on each hand, pecking away like mad. His audience clapped with glee and bought a couple of bags of seed in order to replicate the spectacle.

I was interested in how their attempts would pan out. After a pep talk from the seed seller, one of the girls volunteered herself to be the seed dispenser. Under the seed seller's tutelage, the girl shuffled to a position close to the statue and raised her arms. The man poured some seed into each of her palms. The flock in the puddle stirred but it was a larger group in the trees (including the chest puffer) who swooped first. As the first pigeons began fluttering near her head, the girl screamed and scattered her seed in fright. Two things happened in quick succession: her pals laughed uproariously and every pigeon in Santo Domingo descended on the mess. It was all so predictable.

7

Before Christopher Columbus arrived in 1492, the indigenous population of the island, the Taino, had lived in peace. They had split their domain into five manageable areas, each with its own chief. Under this system of priests, commoners and healers, the Taino people prospered, living off the abundant crops that grew in the fields or the fish they caught in the surf. Then the Spaniards arrived and everything changed.

At first, Columbus described the Taino in positive terms, citing their gentle demeanour and 'lack of evil'. He even wrote in his diaries that they were the nicest people in the world, always laughing and bestowing kindness upon everyone they met. He was also full of praise for their physical appearance, noticing that they were mostly tall and well-proportioned. But these observations did not stop him from exploiting them when he visited for a second time.

On this new visit, Columbus had big plans for the island. First he called it Hispaniola and then established his first base in the Americas there, a settlement he called La Isabella, after the then current Queen. With a town in place, he turned his attention to the Taino people as they smiled and went about their peaceful business. He gathered up the chiefs and demanded they tell their people to deliver to him, free of charge, a regular supply of gold and cotton. If they failed to do so, his men would chop off their hands. And so the chiefs went off to deliver the unpleasant message and later, when some of the Taino failed to bring sufficient amounts of goods, their hands were duly severed at the wrist.

Eventually Columbus left Hispaniola, but more Spaniards arrived, making thing worse for the Taino people. First, they made them toil in the newly-opened gold mines. Bored Spanish soldiers also used the indigenous population as target practice. And then, when food became scarce due to the sudden influx of Europeans, rationing became commonplace. So while the Spanish enjoyed scrumptious meals inside their kitchens, the Taino people starved to death. Against this backdrop, the Taino were also succumbing to terrible diseases against which they had no protection. Measles, influenza and worst of all, smallpox decimated the population and, in just thirty years, the Taino population had almost been wiped out. Today, in small pockets of the Dominican Republic and Puerto Rico, only a few ethnic groups bear any link to the Taino people. Mainly they are of mixed heritage, either Spanish or African. A pure Taino line does not exist anywhere on Earth.

After killing almost every local, and bleeding the country as dry as best they could, the Spanish packed up and moved to their more profitable South and Central American conquests. They kept hold of the eastern portion of Hispaniola but gave the French a section in the west. Both colonial powers immediately replaced the dead Taino with African slaves who, unlike the peaceful Taino, were capable of harder toil.

The statue in the middle of the square was of Christopher Columbus. He was standing on a tall plinth next to a bronze anchor. Columbus looked heroic, pointing into the distance as if pondering his next voyage across the Americas. Below him, climbing the plinth, was a bare-breasted young Taino woman, representing the people his men would eventually wipe out.

Opposite the statue was one of the main tourist draws of Santo Dominica: the Cathedral of Santa Maria la Menor which, at almost five hundred years old, makes it the oldest church in the Americas. It didn't look that old to me, and I wondered how much of it was reconstructed as opposed to original, but it did look striking, especially with the warm yellow hues cast by the morning sun. Built from coral and limestone, it looked more like a castle than a place of worship; clearly Francis Drake had thought the same thing because, when he briefly took over Santo Domingo in 1586, he used the church as his headquarters, inadvertently saving it from the destruction befalling the rest of the city.

It took an eternity to find the entrance to the cathedral; when I did, a pair of elderly American tourists was ahead of me in the queue. Neither of them could work out how to buy entrance tickets because they were both as deaf as posts. No matter how many times the woman behind the counter told them the price in both Spanish and English, they could not grasp it. After an exasperating two minutes of this nonsense, I stepped in and told them. The old man stared at me like I was an apparition, his mouth opening and closing like a haddock. Then the woman asked me to repeat myself, which I did. Finally she nodded in understanding and began a protracted root through her purse to find the exact change. God forbid if she should hand over a couple of cents more than was needed. Behind this buffoonery, I silently seethed.

There is a basic flaw in my personality that gives me no patience in queues when people in front of me are nincompoops, which this pair clearly were. The process of buying a couple of tickets should have taken one minute at most, but this comedy duo had been at it for seven. I almost walked out of the ticket office to storm the barriers, but the thought of being arrested stopped me. Prisons in the Dominion Republic were probably not a good place to be.

I paid for my ticket in ten seconds, passed the doddering slack-jaws and entered the cathedral. Its interior was impressive, full of vaulted arches, long pews, striking glass windows and alcoves full of religious paraphernalia. Not being religious, though, I ambled through everything quickly until I came to a stunning purple-and-blue stained glass window. It had captured my attention due to its unusual subject matter. A dark-robed, sinister man with an upside-down head was flailing his withered arms above a saintly-type man who looked like he was praying. Why the robed man had an upside-down head and why he seemed to be attacking the other man, I had no idea. But clearly the reason was important because someone had made a stained glass window of the event.

In another interesting section, I found a placard. It told me that someone called Rodrigo de Bastidas was buried in the cathedral crypt. As well as having the name of a super cad, Rodrigo was a sixteenth-century Spanish conquistador who discovered Panama but then relocated to Colombia where he was stabbed to death in his sleep. His son, an archbishop, used his religious influence to bring the body to Santo Domingo where he had it interred in the cathedral. With the pensioners fast approaching, I decided it was time to leave and headed back into daylight.

8

I bought a drink and a local newspaper from a tiny shop just off the main square. Then I found a bench again. The plaza was busier now, with plenty more tourists than before. The café was full to bursting and platoons of trinket sellers were wandering around with their beads.

The top story in the newspaper was about thousands of Haitians facing deportation. Half of all Haitians living in the Dominican Republic, the article claimed, were residing without proper documentation and the government wanted them out. Most had arrived in the aftermath of the dreadful 2010 earthquake that killed over 100,000 people and almost destroyed the Haitian capital, Port-au-Prince. With so much devastation in their homeland, it wasn't surprising that so many Haitians had crossed the border in search of aid and a better life. But, seven years on, many had stayed even though their own country was on the mend. They eked out a living picking fruit, gathering crops from the plantations or cleaning people's houses: basically the jobs that no one else wanted. But none of them held any sort of Dominican Republic residency. And this was what the article was discussing: the very contentious issue of illegal Haitians living in the country.

Hospital beds, claimed a medical spokesman, were often taken up by Haitian patients, straining an already-stretched service. According to the spokesman, almost a quarter of pregnant women admitted into Dominican Republic hospitals were Haitian, even though they made up only 7% of the population. Xenophobia is a big issue in the Dominican Republic. 'Immigrants are taking all our jobs' is a common refrain in magazine editorials, inside shops and on the streets of Santo Domingo. The article I was reading was careful not to take sides but it was asking a few good questions. Who would work the fields if all the undocumented Haitians were deported? Who would clean the toilets in the supermarkets and hotels? Who would mow the lawn of the businessman too busy to do it himself? Conversely, it asked what would happen if the health service crumbled under the weight of pregnant Haitian mothers having child after child. And what if these children grew ill – how much strain would they put on the ailing health service? But the most interesting question the article asked concerned all the children born in the Dominican Republic to Haitian parents. Should they be deported, even though they were growing up as citizens in the Dominican Republic? And if they were not sent back, what should happen to them?

They cited a young man who had recently won a place in the Dominican Republic's national boxing team. His parents were justifiably proud; after all, they had paid for him to attend prestigious training centres in his youth and had watched him grow up as a solid citizen of the Dominican Republic. But, because they were Haitians, and illegal immigrants (even though they had lived in the country for over twenty years), the boy was a ghost, unregistered at birth. They had not registered his birth because they knew that if they had done so the authorities would have realised they were illegals. But without this birth registration, the boy had never received a Dominican

Republic identification card: a get-out-of-jail pass that enabled the holder to receive higher education, access to better jobs and, in this boy's case, entry to the national boxing team. It was a similar situation for an eleven-year-old girl who had just finished a Santo Domingo primary school with the highest grades in her class. Without an identification card, she was could not progress to secondary school in order to achieve qualifications to better herself. Her crime: grandparents who were Haitian immigrants.

I closed the newspaper and stuffed it into one of my deep pockets. It was time to hire a guide.

9

I walked purposefully towards a fifty-something guide who was standing by himself. With an immediate smile and a promise of forty-five minutes of walking fun, Hector took me under his knowledgeable wing.

Hector could speak English but his accent was so heavily accented that I could barely understand him. It rendered me a nodding galoot, saying 'yes' and mumbling 'ah, I see', even though I didn't have a clue what he was telling me half the time. Regardless, our first stop was a beautiful square lined with expensive restaurants along one edge and historical buildings along another. The most important building was the former residence of Diego Columbus. It was a block of rectangular stone full of wide arches and deep dark windows: the abode of an important man who not afraid to flaunt his wealth.

"Diego Columbus?" I said. "Not Christopher Columbus?"

"Si. Diego. He was the son of Chreestopher."

Diego Columbus, I later learned, was, like his dad, an accomplished sailor and explorer. After establishing himself as a man of the age, he suddenly found himself, aged just 29, Viceroy of the Indies, which meant moving to Santo Domingo, the key Spanish stronghold in the area. It was a hardship posting, so Diego transported a boatload of his friends and family (including uncles, nieces, cousins and even his old school teacher) to Santo Domingo with him, and then set about building a fine palace that he named the Alcazar de Colon, *Palace of Columbus*. Years later, Francis Drake drove Diego Columbus and the Spanish out and ransacked the palace, tearing out the tapestries, chandeliers and expensive artwork. This left the building a shell of its former self. When the Spanish returned, they didn't have the energy or inspiration to rebuild it and so left it to rot. It was only through the intervention of old dictator Rafael Trujillo that it was restored.

Hector was talking about the exterior, telling me something about coral, which I presumed was what the palace was made from. Then he asked if I wanted to go inside.

"What's in there?"

"Theengs from de homes of de reech people. Pictures, tables and theengs like dat. Maybe you like?"

I doubted it. And so we moved to the oldest street in the Americas: Calle Las Damas, *Ladies Street*. It was the first street the Spanish constructed in the early 1500s, linking their Ozama Fortress to Diego Columbus's palace. It was therefore an important cobbled thoroughfare.

Because of its prime location, many wealthy ladies made their residences along the street, fluttering their eyelashes at the Spanish merchants and naval officers passing beneath their balconies. As well as the eligible young men strolling through, horse-pulled carriages would have clattered along Calle Las Damas, passing the hither and thither of townsfolk peddling spices, salt and pearls. If they had been lucky, the ladies may have caught sight of Diego Columbus making one of his frequent trips between his palace and the fortress.

Nowadays, Ladies Street's grand buildings are tourist shops, museums and something called the Pantheon of the Fatherland which looked like a church, but was actually another mausoleum. When Rafael Trujillo decided he needed a mausoleum, he picked the one along Calle Las Damas. But in the end he needn't have bothered: after his assassination, Trujillo's body was whisked out of the country and sent to Spain.

Inside the pantheon, there was a service going on. There was even a red carpet laid out along the centre where a huddle of dignitaries stood listening to man speaking into a microphone. He was talking in French; he then switched to Spanish; I couldn't understand any of it. I was about to turn tail, thinking I'd gate crashed an official ceremony, when Hector stopped me, telling me that it was okay. He tried informing me what was going on but, due to his accent and the fact he was whispering, I was none the wiser. Still, it was interesting to watch a couple of soldiers dressed in ceremonial blue-and-red uniforms lay a wreath at the front. When they stood still again, it was time to leave. We had a fortress to visit.

10

"This eez named after the Ozama River and not Osama bin Laden," joked Hector, forcing a grin at his own poor joke, one he had undoubtedly told every day of his working life since 2011. We were both staring at the sixteenth-century castle that the Spanish had built to protect their new settlement. It was, according to Hector, the oldest fortress in the Americas.

The Ozama Fortress' main building looked like it belonged in Scotland. Although small in stature, The Tower of Homage possessed a tall turreted tower, holes from where archers could fire, some stout walls (two metres thick, according to Hector) and a big flag on the top. All it was missing was a moat and a portcullis, but it had never needed such things, as the river it overlooked formed the only formidable barrier it needed. It was so sturdily built that no armed force ever breached it, a factor that Rafael Trujillo's regime considered when they used it as a prison until the 1960s.

Today, instead of repelling invaders from the sea or housing criminals, the fortress is a museum piece, one of the first things passengers on cruise ships see as they arrive in port.

Hector and I climbed to the uppermost section of the tower where we gazed out at the Ozama River, a dirty-brown waterway spanned by a few bridges. Moored along the river was a large ferry waiting to take passengers on the twelve-hour journey to Puerto Rica. I asked Hector if he'd ever been there.

"No, never."

"What about Haiti?"

My guide actually laughed. "Why would I go to Haiti? We are rich and they are poor."

"But aren't you interested in seeing what it's like there?"

"No. I know what it's like. Haiti is ugly and dangerous."

I frowned. "But how do you know if you've never been?"

Hector threw me a glance. "From TV and newspapers. Everyone knows what it's like in Haiti. That's why they all come here."

With nothing more to say on the matter, we headed back down the stone steps so we could visit an amber museum.

Walking along Calle Las Damas again, Hector made a phone call. As he spoke to the person on the other end, we turned a corner and arrived in front of a little shop that sold amber products. Hector finished his call. "This is the museum," he told me.

As if on cue, a smiling man emerged from the shop doorway. "Welcome to the Amber Museum," he said.

I shook my head. I told both men that I didn't want to go in. Hector looked crestfallen while the smiling man frowned.

"But this amber museum is part of the tour," said Hector, "I showed you this on information card at the start."

"I know. But I'm not going in. It's not a museum, it's a shop. In fact, I'll be okay from here on. I can make my own way back to the plaza. So thanks for your help." Before he could persuade me otherwise, I paid him his fee, added a little tip and left him and the amber man to ponder their small misfortune.

After a late lunch, I wandered around Santo Domingo's colonial zone, occasionally finding that I had gone in circles, arriving back in the same places. This didn't bother me one bit, because it gave me a chance to see things I might have missed otherwise: a pretty street sign, a tiny abandoned church, a dog scrambling – *Scooby Doo* style – after a bumble bee. Other times, I found myself standing before ruins, including one pile which claimed to be the oldest hospital in the Americas. Santo Domingo, it seemed, was full of the oldest stuff in the Americas: the oldest street, the oldest church, the oldest fort and now the oldest hospital. I gazed through the fence at the pile of remains: open-air arches, broken walls and large pieces of fragmented stonework. If there hadn't been a sign telling me it had been a hospital, I would not have stopped for even a second.

I found myself back on George Washington Avenue, wandering along surely one of the best stretches of ocean in the Caribbean. Even so, despite the dazzling blue water, the creamy sand and the droopy palm trees, my eyes were sagging; when I reached my final sight of the day, a humungous statue taller than three London buses stacked on top of each other, I almost faltered. Forcing my eyes open, I stared upwards at statue of Antonio de Montesino.

Montesino was a sixteenth-century Spanish missionary whose job was to convert the local Taino people into his world of Christianity. As well as this, he had campaigned against the harsh treatment his fellow countrymen were bestowing upon the indigenous population of Hispaniola. Diego Columbus was not impressed with his meddling and shipped him back to Spain, where the missionary somehow managed to persuade the king that protecting the Taino people was in his interests because it was what God would want. In the end, Montesino's efforts were in vain because, as already established, the Taino were wiped out anyway,

Even so, due to his labours, the people of the Dominican Republic erected a statue of Montesino which now stands on a plinth along a fine stretch of Caribbean coastline. The giant missionary looks out across the vastness of ocean towards Venezuela, his final resting place. With one hand cupped over his mouth, it is as if he was shouting to the masses about the ill-treatment of the Taino people.

His statue was a nice way to end my tour of Santo Domingo and, as I walked to my hotel, past the obelisk and the bulldozers (which hadn't moved), I was pleased that the United States had banned me from their country. Without this disqualification, I almost certainly would not have included the Dominican Republic in my itinerary. But here I was, enjoying the cool sea breeze in a city which, prior to my arrival, I had no real knowledge and no inclination to visit.

For the rest of the evening I checked over my flight details, hotel bookings and travel information. The next few days were going to be a carnival of activity. And the next stop was my first nation of Central America: Belize.

SANTO DOMINGO
Top: The statue of Christopher Columbus standing in front of the Cathedral of
Santa Maria la Menor; One of the great beach views along George Washington
Avenue
Middle: The giant statue of Antonio de Montesino; A couple of tourist police
stand chatting in Parque Colon; The Mirabal Sisters' Obelisk
Bottom: Grand tower of the Ozama Fortress; Alcazar de Colon, Diego
Columbus' primary residence when he was in Santo Domingo

Chapter 2. Belize City, Belize

FCO Advice: The majority of muggings are in Belize City. In some areas, there is a risk of gang related violence. Take care walking in the city.

In order to get to Belize from the Dominican Republic, I had to take a flight to Panama City first, and during this first hop, I happened to be seated in an emergency exit row with two empty seats next to me. A young man wearing a Copa Airlines uniform was explaining something to the couple across the aisle. Even though he was speaking in Spanish, I presumed it was instructions about what to do should some sort of emergency occur. I looked at the safety card and it had some instructions in English. The most important one was to know how to fling the hatch out of the window. I could do that, I reckoned, and so when the young man leaned in to speak to me, babbling away in Spanish, pointing to his own safety card and then at the emergency exit window, I nodded and smiled in all the right places, showing full comprehension. Then he finished with a question, which I presumed was something like: *Are you happy with everything and willing to do your duty, sir?*

"Si," I said, nodding. If I had been in possession of some castanets, I'd have clicked them for effect.

Instead of moving on, the man looked confused. Inwardly, I groaned. The young man asked the same question again.

I nodded once more. "Si, señor!" I smiled graciously, even though his question might well have been: *Are you carrying explosives in your hand luggage?* I caught a brief look of pure annoyance.

"You don't speak Spanish, do you?"

I admitted I didn't.

"So why did you not say? I could've said all that in English for you. But I'll start again—"

I cut him off. "I understand what to do in an emergency. Pull this bar here, pull that bar there, pull the door in, twist and throw it out, but not if there's a fire outside or if we're sinking in water."

The young man forced a smile. "Okay, thank you, sir." And with that, he was off to attend to his other, more pleasing, duties.

After my brief stopover in Panama, I was flying northwards towards Belize City. Two hours later, as we began a gentle descent towards the airport, I gazed down upon this little slice of Central America, the only bit that had English as its official language. I couldn't see any mountains to speak of, just an endless bottle-green expanse of grass, dotted with clumps of dense jungle and, occasionally, a brown river or thin dirt road. But if I had been looking through powerful binoculars, I might have spotted a few of the five hundred species of bird and reptile that resided in the untamed lands of Belize. If I was lucky, I might have even spotted an ocelot, a jaguar or a caiman. Howler monkeys were common in Belize, too, as were billions of insects and spiders. The jungle below was positively teeming with nasties such as tarantulas, massive centipedes and black widow spiders, whose venom was fifteen times more powerful than that of a rattlesnake. There was also a two-centimetre-long critter called a bullet ant down there, whose sting was the most powerful in the insect world, akin to being shot with a bullet, hence the name. If we suddenly crashed and I somehow survived (after tossing the emergency hatch outside) but then was unlucky enough to be bitten by a bullet ant, I could look forward to twenty-four hours of 'all-consuming' pain that cycled around mind-warping throbbing, brain-numbing burning, endless groaning and occasional screaming. And these swine lived in colonies of up to three thousand individuals.

But we didn't crash. Instead, we landed at Philip SW Goldston International Airport, the largest airport in Belize. Aside from our plane, the airport only boasted one other passenger jet, an American Airlines Boeing 737 but, as we trundled towards the terminal, I noticed a squadron of smaller, single propeller aircraft parked on the apron. All of them belonged to a small Belizean airline called Tropic Air. I would be boarding one of these planes the next afternoon for my trip to Guatemala. But for now, even if it was for a ridiculously short time, I had Belize to think about.

2

The road leading away from the airport was quiet and tropical; it reminded me of the roads I had seen in some of the Caribbean islands the previous year. Small, brightly-painted homes splashed in yellows, oranges and whites sat amid thick tropical trees. Soaring effortlessly above them, fish eagles scoped out the river on our left. The only downer was a dead dog lying prone by the side of the road. Its beige body showed signs of a major impact. It depressed me for many minutes, even when it had long receded into the distance.

Seemingly in the middle of nowhere, we passed a bar called the Manatee Lookout, which I thought was an excellent name, especially if it was true. The bar's terrace overlooked a section of the thick brown river so I asked the taxi driver about it. "Yeah, you will see manatees there. We have plenty of them in Belize." The driver looked like an old Rasta but his accent was almost American. "Very gentle creatures. But sometimes they get hurt by boats' propellers, you know. You see dead ones floating on the surface of the river from time to time."

We passed a large billboard showing a pair of hands reaching through prison bars. Its slogan read: *Here for child sex tourism? We have rooms for your 12 year stay.* This seedy side of Belize was something I hadn't known about. "Is it a big problem here?" I asked the driver, pointing at the sign.

The man considered the question. "I don't think it's as bad as some places in Asia, but there are some guys who come over here for a sex vacation, and plenty of brothels in the city cater for them. A few of the real bad ones have kids working there, you know. So yeah, we sometimes get sick guys turning up who should stay away, in my opinion."

"Where are they from?"

"The States."

"I'm from England, by the way," I said.

"I guessed that by your accent."

We drove in silence for a while. The scenery was still the manatee river and jungle. "So do you like Belize?" I asked the driver, trying to steer the conversation towards a more agreeable topic.

The man visibly brightened. "I love it. We have everything here: sun, beaches, lots of wildlife, things that work. Don't get me wrong, when I've visited the States, I've enjoyed it, but I much prefer living here. It's a slower pace of life, you know."

We began to approach the outskirts of Belize City, home to just sixty-thousand people. It was one of the smallest places, population-wise I would be visiting. Even so, it was still Belize's largest city, dwarfing the capital, Belmopan, by a factor of three. It contained the main port, most of its banks and businesses, so I expected it to be busy and bustling. But, for a long while, ours had been the only vehicle on the road. Even a large store called Traveller's Liquor LTD seemed empty of patrons, and so did a shop opposite called Sea Shore Store, a name surely hard to pronounce after a couple of beers. Five minutes later, as were reached the more-central parts of Belize City, things began to look a little livelier. I could see people for a start, most just ambling along, or else sitting in doorways, minding their own business. One dreadlocked man, wearing a white T-shirt and denim cut-off jeans, wandered by, a cigarette in one hand and a black plastic bag in the other. Like many men in the Caribbean, his gait was bouncy and measured, his rhythm keeping steady to the beat of Caribbean time.

Parallel to the road was a green sliver of water known as Haulover Creek. The thin river bisected the city and was named after pioneering livestock owners, who took to dragging their beasts across its shallower sections to get to better pasture on the other side.

The pasture was long gone, replaced by wooden huts and, less frequently, breezeblock shacks. Occasionally, a fancy brick house would appear, or a white-painted wooden building; the juxtaposition of styles gave the scene an unmatched flavour, but a nice one nonetheless.

"So this is the city centre?" I commented.

"Yeah, man, this is it. Belize City a quiet place, you know. People come here during the day to work, but at night there's hardly anyone around. So this, right now, is actually busy – but we do have a problem with the population here in Belize. For a country with our landmass, we should have double the people. So there should be more people working here. If it wasn't for all the refugees coming in from Guatemala, El Salvador and Honduras, our population would be going down."

"Why do you think this is?"

He shrugged. "From what I've read, people move to America – but only the educated ones; the States won't let them in otherwise."

"So people get their education here in Belize, maybe get a degree, and then leave on the next plane?"

"Exactly."

"So the classic brain drain."

"That's what I think."

A few minutes later, we pulled up outside my hotel. Belize, here we come.

3

A lot of British people believe that Central America starts at Mexico and ends in Panama. The British education system is to blame for this, constantly stating that Mexico is most definitely part of Central America, sandwiching Guatemala, Belize, El Salvador, Honduras, Nicaragua and Costa Rica with Panama at the bottom, a mini-continent of eight countries. But if a person went to school in Brazil, they would also include Colombia and all the Caribbean nations in this group. Spanish people would scoff at such a notion. In Spain, there is no such thing as Central America (or North or South America for that matter). A child in Spain learns that all the countries in that region, from the tip of Canada to the tail of Argentina are part of one massive continent called the Americas. Even in Central America itself, things are sometimes confusing. Some claim that Belize is part of Central America; some say it isn't, pointing out only Spanish speaking countries can be part of the gang. People from Panama sometimes consider themselves part of South America, and get upset when they are lumped in with the poorer nations further north. Mexico considers itself part of North America, as do all the Caribbean nations. In fact the only countries that do accept that they are in Central American are Guatemala, El Salvador, Honduras, Nicaragua and Costa Rica. I would be visiting them all, but for now I was in Belize, which might or might not have been in Central America, but it looked like it was.

Belize swims alone in a sea of Spanishness, with English lettering everywhere and even its banknotes featuring Queen Elizabeth II. The reason for this lies squarely with Spanish conquistadores' unwillingness to explore the marshy, mosquito-infested lands they found when they sailed across the sea from Cuba. After cutting down some thick jungle and being bitten by bullet ants and tarantulas in the process, they decided enough was enough and left the unforgiving land to roving pirate gangs, the only mariners prepared to set up camp among the swamps. A few decades passed and the British had a look. After throwing out the privateers, they poked around in the jungle with long sticks until one of them discovered an interesting tree. There was a substance contained within its bark that could be extracted to make black dye, a highly-prized commodity in eighteenth-century Europe. And there wasn't just one tree, there were thousands of them. With European dignitaries wanting to shed their jolly red-and-green robes in favour of sombre black robes (especially if they were members of the Spanish Inquisition), these British explorers knew they had found something exciting. So they cleared the jungle vines, swished the mosquitoes away and waited for the African slaves to arrive so they could tend the tree plantations en masse. Belize (or British Honduras as it was soon to be called) briefly became the black dye capital of the world. When other, more readily available, black dyes were found, British Honduras turned to mahogany instead. For the British, this tiny slice of Central America was a real money spinner.

As always, the good times didn't last. An untimely mixture of hurricanes and a fall in demand for expensive wood put British Honduras on the brink. By the 1960s, the British decided to shut up shop and allowed the colony to rule itself. To celebrate, the people of British Honduras renamed themselves Belize and then, in 1981, became a fully independent nation. Since then, Belize has done okay for itself, establishing an economy based upon fruit production, petroleum and tourism. The only thorn in the side, apart from the ever-present threat of hurricanes and bullet ants, is a series of spats with Guatemala over border issues, the same reason the British government kept a military detachment there until 2011.

4

By the time I checked into the hotel and dropped my stuff in the room, it was almost 4 p.m. I had a tour arranged the next morning, but I was itching to get out and see some of Belize City before it got dark.

My hotel was at the tip of a headland that formed one half of Belize City. The Caribbean Sea beyond the peninsular looked choppy and brown, and the few boats tethered to a long jetty were bouncing around in the churn like corks in a bucket. I walked away from the sea to the centre of Belize City, a place of traffic and bicycles, of old US school buses (now regular passenger transporters) and cafés. Bars were commonplace, as were small mama-and-papa stores. I passed a post office and a Chinese takeaway. There were no high-rise buildings and the tallest structure

I could see was an insurance company office. Most of the buildings looked wooden. There was something special about wooden buildings, I felt; they made a town look authentic and lived-in. Belize City was not trying to impress but it was still managing to, just by being there.

I walked past a large shop that had the best slogan in town: *Bottom Dollar*, the store was called, with *Git more fo yer dolla* written underneath. From somewhere, reggae music was blasting out. When I rounded a corner just along from the shop, I found out where it coming from: a small outdoor bar at the other side of the famous Swing Bridge. The bridge was in Belize City's dead centre, a short crossing point where almost every vehicle and pedestrian crossed at some point in a day. First unveiled to the public in 1923, it wowed residents with its novel manner of swinging horizontally across the river on order to allow tall-masted boats to pass unhindered. Back then, four strong men cranked the bridge's machinery by hand twice a day. The same method is used today, making it the oldest swing bridge in the world still operated by hand.

With the reggae music still blasting its way across the river, I walked along the pedestrian-only side of the bridge until I was in the middle. To allow everyone else passage, I pressed myself to the edge to admire the view of the river. Venice it was not, but the surrounds of Haulover Creek were still pretty, albeit in a broken, ramshackle way. One breezeblock building with an unfinished upper storey had white graffiti scrawled on its bare cement wall. Someone called C-Dog had scrawled *Fock you Mam* which must have been pleasant for her to read as she crossed the creek every day.

A couple of gents in beanie hats were sitting outside the bar at the far end, sipping on afternoon beers as they listened to the bass-heavy music. I carried on past them, hitting the shopping district, which contained the only US chain shop in town: Ace Hardware, purveyor of all household goods. Past it was a large white building that proudly declared itself the Belize Bank. It towered over Mule Square, a small triangle of concrete that caught the shadows of the buildings that surrounded it. Once it had been a place for farmers to tether their horses while they traded in the town's markets; nowadays, Mule Square is home to a revolving sign advertising Coca Cola and Belikin Beer.

Perhaps the most magnificent building of the city was the Supreme Court of Belize. It was a grandiose colonial-era white edifice topped with a green roof and a series of freshly-painted, wrought-iron fences along its upper storey. A few people were leaving, chatting as they made their way down the steps leading from the courthouse. None looked like miscreants. In front of the courthouse, near the intersection of Regent Street and Treasury Lane, was an area of green called Battle Field Park. The name of the park was slightly misleading because, as far as I could discern, no battle had ever occurred there, apart from the one the civil council had with the local vagrants who congregated there at night.

But there was one building, above all others, that dominated Belize City, and it was a huge structure called Brodies. It was, by far, the biggest edifice in the city and looked spectacularly uninspiring. But that was because it was a supermarket, albeit a giant one. As soon as I stepped inside its vast network of aisles and displays, the aroma of seasonings hit my senses. In front of me, from left to right, was the largest selection of spices I'd ever seen. It was as if every spice in the world had been bottled, bagged or wrapped in foil and placed in Brodies Supermarket. One section was dedicated to a bewildering array of pepper sauces, some sounding like the foodstuff of the insane. Written on one innocuous little red bottle was a warning in large white capital letters. BEWARE: COMATOSE HEAT LEVEL: HABANERO PEPPER SAUCE.

Hot peppers are rated on something called the Scoville scale. In 1910, Wilbur Scoville, a thin 45-year-old man with a thick shock of dark hair, was working in a Massachusetts laboratory trying to grade the heat of hot foodstuffs into a workable scientific scale. This involved testing a range of spicy things upon his five trained and willing victims. Instead of making his volunteers eat random bits of chilli pepper, Scoville carefully measured an exact weight of a particular chilli, dried it out and then dissolved it in a glass of pure alcohol. After that, he diluted his mixture with a sufficient but diligently-calculated amount of sweetened water and offered it to his test group. If all five testers could detect heat, he added more water in controlled amounts until at least three of them couldn't. By utilising this painstaking approach, Scoville set the standard for measuring the heat of hot foodstuff.

On the Scoville scale, paprika comes in somewhere between 100 and 1000. Most people can cope with paprika, so this is a nice range to start with. Jalapenos, regarded by many as an upper end of heat tolerance, come out at between 2500 and 8000. So, if jalapenos are at 8000, a level of heat where most people start sweating and grabbing at their mouths, how does Tabasco Sauce compare? The ingredient that gives a Bloody Mary its bite packs a respectable punch at 30,000 on the Scoville scale. Not many people could cope with a drop of pure Tabasco on their tongue, which is why only a few drops are mixed into vodka and tomato juice. But even Tabasco is small fry compared to the mighty habanero. These evil chilli peppers are seventy times hotter than Jalapenos, sizzling on the Scoville scale between 350,000 and 580,000. At that heat, the Devil himself is cooking up a storm in a person's stomach. People with high blood pressure or those who have had heart attacks are advised to avoid them. Or else have medical personnel close at hand. Or an undertaker. But even the mighty habanero pepper pales into insignificance next to a demonic chilli called the Dragon's Breath. Grown under strict laboratory conditions in Wales, of all places, this super-hot chilli tops the scale at 2.4 million, which is stronger than police-issue pepper spray. When the mad scientist who spawned the aberration dripped a single drop of chilli juice onto his tongue, the Dragon's Breath chilli immediately turned his face red and caused a cascade of sweat to erupt from every pore of his body. As he ran around in crazy circles, the inside of his mouth burned like it had never burned before. He ended up losing all sensation on his tongue and lips for two days.

As for me, I left all of the chilli pepper sauces well alone and bought some water instead. When I left the store, I found the streets were emptier than before. It seemed the working folk of Belize City were all heading home, which meant it was time for me to return to the hotel.

5

The next day I was up before the sun again. One of the benefits of changing time zones to the west is getting up early. In the UK it was midday, but in Belize, it was only six a.m. Even the screeching of some nocturnal birds had not kept me awake for long the previous evening. After another snooze and then a breakfast that consisted of a Snickers bar, a packet of cheese nachos and two cups of coffee, I felt ready to begin my tour of the city and wandered down to reception to meet my guide. After the tour ended, I would have to return to the hotel to pack for my flight to Guatemala.

"Buenos dias," smiled the young woman behind the hotel counter. Maybe she thought I was Spanish.

"Buenos aires," I replied, my brain fogged by jetlag. The woman glanced up but elected to say nothing, and neither did I. When a stranger says "Good day" and you reply "Good air", something is wrong. I sat down in the foyer instead.

While I waited for my guide, I read a local newspaper called The Belize Times. I liked its snappy slogan: *The Truth Shall Make You Free*. Apart from one story about growing unemployment in Belize, the news concerned a grisly murder. The headline read: *Two Men Chopped*. It described how a couple of friends had been walking home from a night out in Belize City when a third man approached. After arguing about nothing in particular, the third man produced a machete from his pants and proceeded to 'chop' the two young men. One was chopped in the head. He died straight away. The other was chopped in the right side of his neck and survived. The man with the machete ran off into the night, whereabouts unknown.

"Jason Smart?" said a voice with a deep rumble of Americanised Creole. I looked up to see a big man in his mid-thirties. He introduced himself as Julian and I stood up and shook his hand. "So this morning, we'll drive around the city, see what there is to see, stop where we can. Maybe visit a museum if we have time. You ready to go?"

We began a drive through the main streets of Belize City, with Julian pointing out choice buildings such as a girls' school (empty due to the summer holidays), a cricket ground (empty because there was no match) and the home of the Prime Minister, an understated affair for such an important dignitary, I felt. True, it was large and looked well-kept, and it undoubtedly had a great view of Caribbean Sea, but it hardly looked any different to the other nice houses along the coastal strip. There were no armed guards, no barricades and only a standard-issue tall fence. But unlike his neighbours' gardens, the Prime Ministerial residence had a big Belizean flag in the middle of the flowers and grass.

"This is the nicest part of the city," Julian told me from our parked position outside the presidential abode. "Doctors, lawyers, politicians – they all live around here. And because of that, there is little crime – there are too many cameras and security guards for the bad guys to bother trying." I glanced around, looking for guards, but couldn't see any. Instead I took a photo of the street. Julian waited for me to finish, then added, "There might be a little bit of stealing, you know, but no murders or anything like that."

"So Belize doesn't have many murders?" I was thinking of the killing the previous night.

"We have some. They're mainly on the south side of the river. This is the north side. It's the gangs popping one another. Cocaine comes up through Honduras and Guatemala and passes through Belize on its way to the States. The gang bangers get involved in moving it north and fall out and shoot each other. That's the number one cause of murders here in Belize, but the other is jealousy. Some rich guy becomes friendly with his workers. They might be from Honduras and will be poor. They see the boss flashing the cash and they can't resist. They kill him, steal all the money and run back to Honduras. It's a common thing."

I asked about the machete murder I had read about in the newspaper. "Was that on the south side?"

"Yeah, I read about that, too. It was on the south side."

"So I presume we won't be going down there on this tour?"

"We'll be going there – there's a nice church on the south side; some nice shops, too – but we won't be going into any of the gang banger parts…unless you want to?"

I sniggered. "I don't think so."

Julian checked his watch. "Are you sure? How about we take a drive down there now so you can see what it's like. At this time of the morning, it'll all be good. All the bad guys are asleep."

"So it's not dangerous?"

"At night, hell yeah! But now, it will be fine."

And so, against all Foreign Office advice, our car headed for the south side of the creek.

6

We turned away from the coast and drove along a thin road that intersected an even thinner road: more a track, really. Even though the dwellings were still some distance away, it was clear it was a shanty town. Low-lying electricity wires dangled over the scattering of shacks. I couldn't see any people, but that was because we were too far away. Julian stopped the car at the intersection regarding the district. Once again, I asked him whether it was safe for us to drive through. "No problem. Look, if a bad guy comes out, we run like hell." He laughed at his own comment. And so we set off towards the homes of street robbers and gang bangers.

Most of the shacks looked half-finished or, if they had ever been finished, then they were in a state of major disrepair. Tin roofs, crumbling walls, old wooden panels and slatted windows without glass made up the vast majority of the buildings. Rubbish was everywhere, piled up in dirty gardens or littering the trees. It was as if the residents had deemed their little pocket of Belize City not even worthy of a clean-up. As well as the litter, broken pieces of wood sat in untidy piles next to rotting cars bereft of doors and wheels. Clothes hung from wire outside the shacks. A woman with a baby was sitting in one doorway; a man pushing a cart of fried food passed her and waved. Everywhere was down at heel; even the thin strip of water running parallel to the road looked like it was being used as a dump site.

"All these homes are owned by the people living in them," Julian mentioned. "Under Belizean law, anyone who has squatted in the same place for fourteen years gets to keep the house, and that's what most of these people have done."

"So apart from the drug dealers, is everyone here unemployed?"

"Some, but most are working. They might be immigrants working on farms, or single mothers relying on their extended family. Early in the morning, they'll walk to rich people's houses and clear their yards for a few dollars, or maybe they'll see if there's anything going on at a construction sites. Life's tough for them, man; prices are high in Belize but wages are low. But do you know something?" Julian pointed to our right. It was another group of two-storey hovels with tyres holding down tin roofs. "See all the washing machines and fridges?"

I could. On the upper level of almost every dwellings, resting on sparse verandas, were white goods. And unlike the houses to which they belonged, the machines looked brand spanking new. I looked at Julian quizzically.

"I know – it seems odd, doesn't it? And inside each house you'll find new 34-inch TVs. So, even though these people are poor by most standards, they are still doing okay. They have enough dough to buy nice things and pay for the electricity to power them."

"So what about the gangs?"

"What about them?"

"Do they control things around here, like they do in El Salvador and Honduras?"

"No, nothing like that, man; they're too disorganised. They're just a bunch of young guys. Being in a gang offers them some respect. They see the gang bosses with their nice cars, the girls on their arms, the gold necklaces, and they want some of that. We have two main gangs here in Belize City: the Bloods and the Crips. If there's a murder, ninety percent of the time it's one of them killing the other. The Bloods wear red and the Crips wear blue. If you see a guy wearing mainly those colours, then he will probably be part of a gang. That's why I'm wearing a black T-shirt."

My shirt was blue. I asked whether people might think I was a member of the Crips.

Julian sniggered. "No way, man. For one, you're too old: most of the gangbangers are young guys, maybe teenagers and early twenties. And second, you're a white guy: all the Bloods and Crips are black guys."

I asked which gang area we were driving through. I was scanning the houses for any sign of young men wearing blue or red. None fitted the bill. In fact, there were no young people at all. Perhaps they were, as Julian had suggested, all tucked up in bed.

"The Crips run this area. But the gang boundaries are not solid, and sometimes the areas cross over. I was reading about something that happened a few days ago, actually. Some guy was working as a barber not far from here. I don't think he was part of a gang or anything but he was regularly cutting a Bloods dude's hair. Word got around and some Crips heavies came into his shop, telling him not to cut the guy's hair again. But he must've ignored the warning and so some gang banger blasted him with a shotgun. This was a month ago, but the guy survived, that's what I was reading about. He can't walk or talk anymore and his family can't cope. All because he cut the wrong guy's hair."

7

Back in the centre of town, I realised I had been to the south side of the river already. The previous evening, when I had crossed the Swing Bridge, I had been wandering amid prime danger. Brodies Supermarket, ACE Hardware, Battle Field Park were all on the south side. The main road of the city, Albert Street, was busy with shoppers, men on bicycles and stout female police officers directing traffic. One store called Wellworth sold household goods at the lowest prices possible but at the best quality.

"So is there anything bad about living in Belize?" I asked Julian. He had already told me that the best thing was the weather.

"Corruption," he answered immediately. "It's what holds Belize back. It starts with the policeman wanting a backhander when you run a light, all the way up to people in the government. And it's rooted in three things: land, immigration and greed. Land because people always need to build a factory or a timber yard somewhere and they're prepared to pay a bribe to get the best plot. With immigration, it's about Hondurans and Salvadorians staying here illegally. People turn a blind eye as long as the immigrants pay them. But politicians are the worst. That's where greed comes in."

I nodded, telling Julian that I had heard the same thing said about many countries. "But I've often wondered something," I said. "I know corruption's bad, but if I was in the government and someone offered me a pile of cash to sign a piece of paper, I wonder if I could say no. It takes a special sort of person who can say no to that, especially if he has a family to feed."

Julian was nodding and smiling. "Yeah, I've wondered that too. And so did the old prime minister – a guy named Said Musa. He was as corrupt as the best of them, but when he left office, he said something to the guy who took over. The new guy was moaning about how corrupt the old Prime Minister was and how he was going to be different. After a few arguments back and forwards, Musa told him to stop throwing stones. He said it was easy to be pious when the meals he was eating were tacos and cheese. He should wait until he was eating filet mignon and lobster and then see if he still had rocks to throw."

It was a good analogy, I thought.

"But the only time I heard that someone could not buy off an official was when some religious group came to Belize and asked the government for some land so they could build a church and a runway. The government asked why they needed a runway and they said it was for visiting alien spaceships. Even the government said no to that."

Julian pulled over along the busy street. On one side was a strikingly white place of worship called the Wesley Methodist Church; on the other was a long orange-and-red building called the Wesley Lower School. Close to it was a small Hindu temple, also in white but decorated with pastel orange decorations. I was surprised by its presence, but Julian explained that many Hindus lived in the city; most of them had moved to Belize in the 1950s when the country had been part of the British Commonwealth.

"And do people in Belize accept them?"

Julian glanced at me. "What do you mean?"

"I mean, is there any racism in Belize?"

"No. There is no racism. Many of the Indians own textile shops in the city. We will pass a few later on today. And we have Chinese, and people from the Middle East, too. Good luck to all of them."

Further along Albert Street, just down from a branch of the Atlantic Bank and a stately-looking law firm called Barrow and Williams, was Belize City's prime tourist hotspot: St John's Cathedral. Scores of people with large hats and bright dresses or, in the case of the menfolk, suits and ties, were walking up the stone path into its entrance. Since it was Saturday morning, I concluded that there was a wedding or possibly a funeral about to take place.

St John's was not as pretty as the Methodist church up the road. Instead of sparkling white, its exterior was made up of dull-brown bricks. The British designed the church but it was the toil of slaves that had built it, and they did a good job because it had withstood every hurricane and fire that bore down upon it since its grand opening in 1820. The only thing missing was the original spire. But I guessed the people of Belize City could live without it.

I climbed out of the car, leaving Julian to make a phone call, and walked around the cathedral, nodding to the people heading inside, including a small boy wearing shorts and braces. Around the other side, I could hear the sea; I couldn't see it, though, because a large clump of trees and a few nondescript buildings blocked it from view. And then I found a little triangular parcel of land bounded by a children's play area, an old cemetery and a two-storey structure called Southside Meats. In the centre of the triangle was an unusual statue surrounded by bushy palms. The statue was made not of bronze or copper but of painted concrete.

The placard told me it was Isiah Emmanuel Morter who, judging by his representation, was a distinguished gent who enjoyed wearing black suits and bow ties. Morter's expression was curious, though: his eyes were wide like eggs, as if he'd witnessed something terrible, which might well have been true, since he was descended from slaves brought over from Nigeria. But I doubted that was the reason, since most things in Morter's life had been okay. During the late nineteenth century, following the abolition of slavery, Isiah Morter found himself growing up a free man. After saving up a small sum of money, he bought himself a few acres of fertile soil in which to plant some coconuts. Then he sat back and waited for them to grow. They did and, when he had picked and sold everything, he found himself with a small profit, which he ploughed back into buying more land. And so it went on until, eventually, Morter was growing so many bananas and coconuts that he became British Honduras' first black millionaire. When people saw him passing in his carriage, they called him the Coconut King.

Back in the car, I questioned Julian about the Coconut King.

"Who?"

"The Coconut King, Isiah Morter."

"Oh, you mean that statue around the corner. Yeah, I remember now. Not too many tourists see that statue because it's in not a good area. The Bloods run that part. But yeah, he's famous for growing coconuts, I think."

And with that, we headed back up Albert Street to finish our tour on the northern side of the river.

8

After a drive over the Swing Bridge, our final stop was the Museum of Belize. Prior to being a museum, it was the city's prison, which accounted for its heavily-gated, arched entrance. I left Julian in his car and walked through the arch until I found a helpful woman inside the entrance. She gave me some information about where things were in the museum. "Most people find the slave section the most interesting." I thanked her and walked past an array of pots, bottles and beads. Some of the bottles had once contained bush medicines: Blue Flower, which had supposedly 'eased constipation and skin irritations'; Cerasee Tea was 'used to fend off worm infections and malaria', whereas China Root was 'used as a blood builder etc.' What the et cetera stood for, I had no clue.

I came to a section of the museum which had a few information boards about some of the former inmates. Randolph Harris, I read, was executed in 1955 for murdering his wife with an ice pick. His motive: doubt over the paternity of his children. Terrence Cain was executed the same year for stabbing a woman twenty times with a six-inch blade. His motive: a misunderstanding. Some misunderstanding.

Upstairs was a room full of dead bugs. Inside large display cabinets were colourful butterflies tacked onto boards with tiny pins. Next to them were large flies, massive beetles and tarantulas. One insect in particular gave me cause for concern. It was over an inch in length with a black body, orange-spotted wings and a long, thin head section. It didn't look dangerous, but it was. It was a deadly triatomine bug.

These little beauties wait in the shadows of a person's bedroom, perhaps in between a mattress or in the folds of a jumper, waiting until it is dark and their intended victim is asleep. Due to their habit of silently landing on a person's face and sucking up a blood meal (similar to how mosquitoes feed), they are often called kissing bugs. They suck up so much blood that their little bellies become bloated. So to make room they defecate on the person's face. And it is in these tiny piles of insect poo that a nasty parasite called Trypanosomiasis cruzi lurks. When the victim wakes up, long after the kissing bug has departed, they find an irritating itch which they naturally scratch, inadvertently rubbing the parasite into the wound. And then they might catch Chagas disease (comically pronounced Shagger's disease).

But there is nothing funny about Chagas disease. It has two distinct phases. The first is an initial acute stage where the sufferer experiences bad headaches and possibly vomiting. For most people, this phase is as bad as it gets, but for others (reportedly up to thirty percent), the second phase kicks in: the parasites hide in the body's cells, especially the ones in the heart, brain and digestive system, where they bide their time.

Decades later, with the patient utterly unaware of the hidden parasites enjoying a Chagas party inside their organs, the disease decides to act. Some of the parasites escape the cell walls in which they have been hiding and flow freely into the bloodstream. As they swim around, they arrive at the heart, where they cause severe inflammation which can sometimes cause cardiac arrest and death. Those with digestive problems find it hard to eat. Some people have died of malnutrition due to the Chagas parasite.

And these kissing bugs live in a geographical area that extends from South America into Central America and up into some of the southern United States. It is estimated that, at any one time, eight million people have the parasite living in their cells, waiting for the day the shaggers come to town. Every years, thousands die from it. And there is no cure. But imagine ringing up work: "Sorry, I can't come in today; I've got Shagger's disease; I've been up all night." It was almost worth catching the disease just to say that. After checking the corners of the room for live kissing bugs, I went off to find information about slaves.

Slaves in Belize, after toiling in the logging fields all day, were fed a diet of pork and bread, sometimes supplemented with plantains and yams. Whatever was left after a meal was boiled up to make a second meal of the day. For added flavour, some enterprising slaves would add pig's tails or onions. But that was where the fun ended. One large display described the cruelty of the British towards their slaves. One British landowner, a man called Thomas Black, ran a logging plantation. When he found one of his slaves 'malingering', he whipped him to death. In court, he pleaded not guilty because no one had told him it was against the law to whip his own slave. In a rare gesture of justice, the jury found him guilty of the killing, fined him one hundred pounds, took his land and banished him from British Honduras for three months.

Another case of slave cruelty involved a woman called Peggy. Her owner, a man who went by the name of Doctor Mansfield Bowen, was particularly vile. After finding some of his favourite handkerchiefs missing, Bowen accused Peggy and, without waiting for anyone to contradict him, he tied and whipped her until she was half dead. When Peggy's husband found her, he offered to pay for the missing handkerchiefs so that he could untie and tend her wounds. For some reason, this peace offering enraged Dr Bowen so much that he untied Peggy, dragged her into his rat-infested barn and shackled her inside. Five days later, with no sight or sound from Peggy, he finally allowed the husband to release her. Miraculously, she was still alive, and the pair staggered straight to the authorities to lodge an official complaint.

The British magistrates made their notes, nodded their heads and then sent Peggy and her husband on their way, informing them that they would investigate the matter. But, in the meantime, Dr Bowen caught wind of the allegations and dragged Peggy to a public post and stripped her naked below the waist. Then he ordered three slaves to whip her while he watched. He was clearly deranged and was not afraid to show it.

During the subsequent trial against him, Peggy, her husband and the three slaves who had whipped Peggy were all asked to give evidence, which they did. Each of them told the court the same thing: that Peggy had suffered massively at the hands of Dr Bowen. Again, the magistrates nodded their heads and considered the testimony. It was an open-and-shut case but since, according to British Law, the testimony of a slave could not be counted as evidence in a court of law, Mansfield Brown was acquitted of any wrongdoing.

Shaking my head at the pathetically inadequate judicial system during the days of the Belize slave trade, I left the museum and found Julian. It was time to return to the hotel.

9

After lunch, I decided to go for another solo wander. This time, instead of walking into the city, I headed north to the sea. It still looked brown and soupy, with heavy sediment stirring within its depths due to the swell. A few grey pelicans were flying above the waves close to a boat tethered to the end of a thin pier.

I walked around a small headland that led me towards a spindly red-and-white-striped lighthouse. To my left was the sea; to my right, clumps of palms trees dotted around a few circular benches. A young couple were sitting on one and, when they noticed me, both waved. I waved back, thinking about the people who avoided Belize City due to perceived – and in my opinion, unwarranted – danger levels.

The Baron Bliss Lighthouse dates from 1885, named after a wealthy British man called Henry Bliss who, despite being British, had somehow inherited a Portuguese noble title due to his late father's dealings in Europe. After suffering from polio, Henry Bliss found himself wheelchair-bound, but managed to travel around the Caribbean in his specially adapted boat. With his wonderful collection of sailor's caps, Bliss initially settled in the Bahamas, then dropped his anchor in Trinidad and Jamaica and finally arrived in British Honduras in 1926. By then he was very ill and the harbour was the closest he got to dry land; he slept on his yacht, venturing out on the odd occasion for fishing trips. Still, he must have enjoyed British Honduras because, when he died a couple of months later, he left his considerable fortune to the government there, on the proviso that they carry out a couple of requests: he wanted to be buried on the mainland and every year the city had to host a regatta. The government not only accepted these conditions, they went a couple of steps further. After they buried Bliss, they built a lighthouse and named it after him. Then they declared 9th March a public holiday called Baron Bliss Day. Nowadays, the holiday continues as National Heroes and Benefactors Day. But the Baron Bliss Regatta continues.

I stared at the tomb of Henry Bliss. It lay beneath the lighthouse. It was made from black granite and surrounded by a painted iron fence. I smiled as I gazed upward. The lighthouse was a fitting memorial to a man who had loved the ocean so much.

With a few specks of rain making their presence known, I walked back to the hotel, pleased I'd stopped in Belize City on my way to Guatemala. It would have been so much easier, logistically, to have missed it out and gone straight to Guatemala. Speaking of which, Flores was the next stop on my journey. After a short flight in a tiny plane belonging to Tropic Air, it would be time to see some prime Guatemalan Maya history.

BELIZE CITY
Top: Supreme Court of Belize behind a well-placed sign; Looking dapper in
my tropical surrounds
Middle: People heading over the famous Swing Bridge; The Baron Bliss
Lighthouse; St John's Cathedral – Belize City's main tourist draw
Bottom: Isiah Emmanuel Morter, the Coconut King; One of the poorer districts
of Belize City; Hot pepper sauce made with habanero peppers

Chapter 3. Flores, Guatemala

FCO Advice: Guatemala has one of the highest crime rates in Latin America. There is a low arrest and conviction rate. Victims have been killed resisting attack.

Under a dull grey sky, I arrived at Belize's small international airport to find it packed with American passengers. Saturday was the busiest day for flight arrivals and departures, and most of the airport seats were taken up by American folk waiting for their flights to Dallas, Houston or Miami. The Tropic Air gate was tucked at the end of the departure terminal, which was where I was waiting for my early-evening flight to Flores in Guatemala. While I waited for it to be called, I decided to pay a visit the toilet. And it was in these toilets that I came to consider something I had never considered before.

A small sign read: *Please do not use your foot to flush the toilet.* In all my time of using public toilets, I had never once thought about using my foot to flush the toilet. But what a good idea, I thought. Flushing with a foot eliminated the need for my hand to come into contact with potentially deadly germs. And the more I considered this new notion, the more I deemed it acceptable for my own purposes. I inspected the flushing lever. It was a standard side-issue metal hinge and looked sturdy enough to handle footwear. I decided to give it a try. Lifting my foot to the lever, I pressed down and heard the satisfying rush of water. Thank you Belize Toilet Authorities for this top tip: you are toilet gods.

Back in the terminal, I saw the sky darken further; ten minutes later, I heard the first rumbles of thunder. This was closely followed by a wave of rain hitting the windows. Almost immediately, Belize Airport went into shutdown mode. Doors leading outside were closed, people with walkie-talkies busied themselves with conversation and, on the information boards, all-upcoming flights were now reported as DELAYED. The Houston passengers were kicking up a stink as they had been about to board their aircraft.

"Why can't we go?" asked an American man. A fair enough question, I thought. I waited to hear the gate agent's response.

"Thunder and lightning, sir."

"So what? Other airports have lightning storms and carry on."

"No air bridge, sir. No unauthorised personnel allowed airside. Everyone must wait until the all-clear is given."

Passengers tutted and sighed, but found seats in which to ride the storm. As for me, I checked the Tropic Air information screen and saw that every flight was delayed by at least twenty minutes. I found a space at the back of the terminal (one of the few available spaces) and started to read a book on my phone. Above the roof of the airport, the storm continued, booming, flashing and shaking the foundations like an enraged Maya god.

Fifteen minutes later, the storm subsided enough for the walkie-talkie brigade to kick into urgent action. Then a door opened and the Houston passengers departed. As they did, a muffled Tropic Air announcement sounded. A troop of passengers rushed to the gate and left. Another Tropic Air flight was called and then departed and I became worried. Maybe I'd missed my boarding call. I went to the Tropic Air counter and presented myself. When the man behind the counter asked where I was going, he told me my flight to Flores was due to leave in about ten minutes. I thanked him and returned to my wall.

Someone tapped me on the shoulder. It was the Tropic Air service agent I'd spoken to earlier. "Your flight is ready now, sir. Please follow me."

I was impressed. Personal service was something I could get used to, even though I wondered where the other passengers were. Outside, I was even more impressed when I was passed to another Tropic Air agent wearing an orange high-visibility vest. The new man wanted to see my boarding card. "Okay, Mr Smart," he said. "Follow me to the aircraft. You're the only passenger on this flight."

"The only passenger?" That had never happened to me before.

"Yes, sir."

While I took this news in, I followed the ramp agent towards the small plane. "So if I'm the only passenger, if I hadn't booked a seat, would it have still gone?"

"Yeah. They would've flown the first sector empty. They are picking up some passengers to bring back here."

"I see."

I smiled to myself. I had a plane to myself. This was a taste of a real millionaire lifestyle.

2

The two pilots were busy with their pre-takeoff checks. I watched them because there was no cockpit door: they were simply sitting in front of me. I chose one of the twelve empty seats and strapped myself in, still blinking at my good fortune; to be flying in a plane with more pilots than passengers seemed ridiculous. I looked at the sky and saw the grey was thinning to white. The rain had almost stopped.

Take-off was bumpy, especially in such a small single-propeller plane, but soon the three of us were through the worst of it, cruising at 14,000 feet in calm air. A quarter of the way into the forty-five minute flight, I spied a large village on the left. Except it wasn't a village, it was Belmopan, capital of Belize.

Belmopan is one of the smallest capital cities in the Americas, and one of the youngest. Sick of hurricanes and waves battering Belize City, the government decided a new capital was needed, and the location they picked was inland and on a hill to avoid any potential flooding. Work began in 1967 and was completed three years later. The problem was that most people were reluctant to move there, especially business owners and hoteliers who had established their livelihoods in the old capital. Ordinary citizens didn't want to move either, but the Belizean authorities pushed forward with their plans anyway, resulting in a situation whereby Belmopan, the capital, is dwarfed by Belize City. But if I wanted to visit places such as the Belize Immigration Department or the Belize Ministry of Education, then Belmopan was the place to be. Ministries aside, the new capital does have one incredible plus on its side: the road that leads away from it is the excellently named Hummingbird Highway, reportedly one of Central America's prettiest stretches of road.

With Belmopan disappearing behind the plane's left wing, Google Maps informed me that we had crossed over into Guatemalan airspace. Guatemala looked identical to Belize: thick, luxuriant jungle clustered around small lakes. The pilots weren't interested in the lakes or the trees; they were looking to their left where a series of cumulonimbus clouds towered. The captain periodically checked his visual observations with his computer weather map screen. The clouds outside were thunderclouds, which was why the pilots were studying them. They were too far away to cause us any trouble, but on the return journey, depending upon the wind direction, they might be something to think about.

Because I had the passenger cabin to myself, and the windows inside Tropic Air's Cessna Caravan were larger than the standard-issue passenger jet windows, the approach into Mundo Maya International Airport, a grand name for what was essentially a one-stop landing strip, was supremely satisfying. Gone was the drizzle of Belize, replaced by the gorgeous evening sunshine of wild Guatemala. With the runway visible through the cockpit windshield, I allowed my gaze to alternate between the airport and the surrounding landscape, which was mainly a large body of water caressed by thick vegetation. The water belonged to Lago Peten Itza, Guatemala's second largest lake and, as we came in for final approach, I spied the island of Flores in the middle. I would be staying in a hotel there the next evening. A small crop of densely-packed, mostly red-roofed buildings was whizzing underneath the

Cessna's wing. And then we were down in the third country of my trip.

3

The only planes at the airport were other light aircraft, even smaller than ours. While the pilots shut down the engine and turned everything off, I shouted thanks to them. They both turned and nodded. Outside, I waited for my luggage, but an airport worker said I couldn't take it.

"Why?"

"Security reasons, señor. I have to carry it in."

I shrugged and walked to the airport terminal, feeling a little foolish as I did so. As I was the sole arriving passenger, it seemed as if the airport had remained open just for me. This notion was cemented when I entered the small terminal. Sitting inside a small booth was a uniformed woman armed with a computer and an ink stamp. And behind her were two men waiting to check my bag, which hadn't arrived yet. With a stamp in my passport, I moved towards the two men who looked at me expressionless. The immigration officer was already leaving.

"Hola," I offered to the security men.

The men nodded. One returned the greeting; the other looked beyond me, saying something to the two Tropic Air pilots walking through the terminal. All three clearly knew one another. When my bag arrived, the security men asked me to open it. I did so and they glanced at my tightly-packed clothes.

"Any contraband?" one asked.

"Only a couple of small bottles of wine."

He nodded and the men had a quick rifle through the bag. "Okay, that's fine. You can close your bag. Welcome to Guatemala,"

I thanked him, took my bag and walked to arrivals. Waiting for me was a man with my name written on a sign. Since I was the only passenger, it seemed a little unnecessary but I smiled and pointed to myself anyway.

I shook hands with Xavier, who was going to drive me northwards to my jungle lodge. As we headed to his car, I noticed the pilots heading towards the departures building next door. They could look forward to the same immigration process in reverse in order to fly back to Belize City.

Xavier, in his early thirties, was a man of few words, I soon discovered. He had traditional Maya features and could speak a little English, but not enough for a decent conversation; with my Spanish even worse, we set off on our journey to Tikal, base camp for the Maya ruins, in silence. Even when a wild horse ran into the road, stood in our lane and shuffled its hooves, Xavier did not speak. He brought us to a standstill, switched on his hazard lights and waited for the wild beast to move away, which it did after a few seconds.

After passing by a sizeable army base, guarded by sentry towers, barbed wire and an old jet fighter painted with snarling teeth, we hit rural Guatemala. Rolling hills, tropical vegetation, snuffling piglets, loitering dogs, pecking chickens and kids playing football by edge of the lake were some of the sights. Occasionally I'd see swamp land surrounded by deciduous trees but, for the most part, it was thick green palm leaves. The scenery reminded me of somewhere in South East Asia, maybe Indonesia or Vietnam. A chicken bus passed in the opposite direction, a festival of bright green and yellow, finished with an impressive array of chrome fittings and lights. Chicken buses were ubiquitous in Central America, plying all the popular routes, usually at top speed and crammed with passengers. This one was no different and left a swirl of dust eddies in its wake.

Our simple two-lane highway occasionally ran through tiny villages. Each one looked the same as the last: a small restaurant, a bare-chested man riding a push bike, a series of haphazardly-parked cars and thick clumps of palm trees. I saw another couple of horses loitering by the side of the road; I tried to spot their owner, but it appeared they had a free rein to wander where they liked.

Horses are popular in Guatemala, and to own one is a great honour. In plenty of Guatemalan towns, festivals are held which involve horses; the most famous one takes place in Todos Santos, a small town up in the mountains close to the Mexican border. Every year, to celebrate Guatemala's victory over Spain, the men of the Todos Santos drink as much booze as they can before donning feather hats and flouncy clothing. Then, utterly drunk and incapable, they climb upon their steeds and race each other. Some riders are so intoxicated that spectators have to tie their hands to the reins so they won't fall off. Others are not drunk enough and clutch cans of beer as they race around a specially-constructed dirt track. Predictably, despite the safety precautions, a few drunken riders fall and injure themselves, sometimes severely. Particularly unlucky ones have broken their necks or have been trampled by opponents' horses.

Xavier spoke, gesturing to the front. "Many ... blockages ..."

He was right. A series of cyclists, about fifty of them, were in the road ahead, sometimes two or three abreast. It looked like a race. We, along with a truck carrying melons, had no choice except to follow their procession. Every now and again, thank God, we managed to leapfrog a few riders, and when we did, I noticed that each one possessed a professional-looking bike, plus the standard-issue Lycra top and shorts. The only problem was that most of them were lard asses. Rolls of fat bulged out from their tight Lycra as they heaved themselves along the road. Only at the very front of the pack – and leading by a considerable margin – were the lean athletes. Once past them, we roared off along the highway.

We passed a makeshift police roadblock. It was next to a stand selling coconuts and a shack selling burritos. A couple of officers were standing next to the burrito stand. They watched as we approached; I was sure they were going to stop us, but they didn't; one of them just waved us through. With the roadblock receding behind us, I asked Xavier whether the police in Guatemala were fair and just; his answer was a knowing shrug.

"So they're corrupt?"

"Maybe."

With the sun almost down, I noticed another roadblock ahead. It belonged not to the police but the Tikal National Park security. They wanted to check that I had a ticket for the park (I did: I'd bought it at the airport when I had arrived) and so we drove on, along a thin road cutting through dense jungle. Every now and again, we passed yellow diamond-shaped road signs that warned of animals that could suddenly spring out from the trees: snakes, turkeys, racoon-like mammals called coatis and, best of all, jaguars.

I asked Xavier whether he'd ever seen a jaguar. He shook his head. He then elaborated in a rare display of conversation. "I thirty years old and have driven this road hundred, maybe thousand times. I not see one jaguar."

For the next ten minutes, I peered outside in the vain hope of seeing a large spotted cat, but it was a pointless task; in the short time it had taken us to drive away from the park entrance, the sun had already disappeared over a western horizon. The Guatemalan jungle outside was a wall of impenetrable black.

4

"Welcome to the Jaguar Inn, amigo," said the middle-aged man behind the reception desk. His desk doubled as a bar. Five minutes previously, Xavier had driven me through a dimly-lit, but less jungle-like, area of the national park. Aside from an empty car park, the tiny settlement possessed a visitors' centre (closed and dark) and a couple of empty craft stalls. Just off from them was a thin dirt track that led to one of the three lodges where people could stay. At the end of the track was the Jaguar Inn, the mid-priced choice of the trio. It featured a range of jungle huts, a small swimming pool and a large thatched reception building that also served as the hotel restaurant. A few hardy travellers were having drinks while poring over guidebooks and maps.

The manager said, "It's approaching 7 p.m. right now, which means you've just over two hours of electricity and water left. By 9 p.m., most people around here are getting ready to sleep because there's no power. At 6 a.m. it will come back on, but only for three hours, then for the rest of the day, no electricity. But that is life in the Guatemalan jungle."

I picked up the hefty room key and asked him about an evening meal. I was starving; the last thing I had eaten was a Snickers bar in Belize Airport.

"We're open for another hour. So don't worry. You can grab a couple of beers, too."

It sounded good but, as I was about to leave, the man spoke again. "I've just checked your booking; you're in one of our specials. You paid extra for it. We're trialling something at the moment during the low season. When all the power goes off in camp at nine, the special rooms like yours should – I say should, because, like I said, this is all a bit experimental – keep some power. We've installed some back-up batteries that should keep your lights and fan working. You'll find out at 9 p.m., I suppose. Fingers crossed, amigo."

I thanked him and toddled off in the near-darkness to my lodge, listening to the cascade of insect calls and distant monkey sounds. It took ages to manhandle the mediaeval-sized key into its slot, but when I did, I opened the door and surveyed my accommodation for the night. Despite the hefty price tag, the room was stark: functional rather than pleasing. But it did have an adequate bathroom and a big fan that shook the ceiling when I switched it on. When a fearsomely large beetle scurried across the floor and hid underneath a wooden unit, I knew I had well and truly arrived in the jungle. After scanning the mattress for kissing bugs, I headed back to the main building.

My meal was fine, washed down with a couple of bottles of Gallo beer. And then afterwards, back in my room, I awaited the stroke of nine with a sense of trepidation. The air was already muggy; if the fan stopped working, my night promised to be uncomfortable. I grabbed the hotel-provided torch in case the lights went out and put it on the bedside table. As well as providing light, it would make a hardy weapon should the beetle decide to mount a night time attack.

With a couple of minutes still to go, I checked every nook and cranny for signs of kissing bugs. There were none to be found, but I noticed plenty of dead insects in the metal window screens. Most had perished trying to force their way through the tightly-woven mesh. They looked disgusting: miniature insectile zombies.

And then the lights went out.

The darkness was immediate and complete. Then, barely a second later, a sound fizzed and whirred and the lights flickered back to life. The fan sped up again and all was well. I poured myself a glass of wine in celebration and read about Tikal.

5

Tikal, of course, is Guatemala's prime site for Maya ruins, a once-thriving community of one hundred thousand citizens. They lived about two thousand years ago and the city did so well, in fact, that it became a victim of its own success. Overpopulation meant arable land dwindled, as did the city's scant water supplies. When more people arrived in the city of plenty, they strained resources further, and then tribal fighting added another nail to the coffin. Suddenly Tikal was not the place to be and people started leaving. By 900 A.D., everyone had packed up and left. In their wake, jungle vines and creepers tentatively reached the outlying temples and structures, covering the steps with root and leaf. And over the course of the next few decades, thicker roots coiled around the statues and altars. Cracks formed, sections broke off and the jungle encased it all. Apart from by a handful of knowledgeable locals, the vast array of temples, pyramids, carvings and statues was forgotten: just another overgrown part of the Guatemalan rainforest. And so it remained for the next eight hundred years, with only the occasional farmer venturing into the old city to trap animals or to plant crops.

Fast forward to 1848, and a group of intrepid explorers are setting off into the jungles of northern Guatemala armed with large machetes, sketchpads and little else. The band of braves is led by a 48-year-old moustachioed man with thick and lengthy sideburns; he is Modesto Mendez, a local boy from Flores, now a decorated war hero and explorer. As Mendez and his collection of merry men make their way northwards, battling through thick and unforgiving terrain, fighting off jaguars, alligators, pythons and kissing bugs, they somehow stumble upon the old ruins of a Maya megacity. Wiping the sweat away from his brow, Modesto Mendez ordered everyone to stop so that the man with the sketchpad could draw the scene. When the sketch was finished, Mendez looked from drawing to ruin and back again before nodding assent. Then the explorers set up camp for the night and, the next morning, after one final lingering look at the massive jungle-infested temples, they returned to Flores to tell people what they had found.

Nobody cared.

And so nothing much happened for the next five years, until a German newspaper caught wind of Mendez's discovery and printed an article. The article was accompanied by a copy of the artist's drawing which – quite frankly – looked like a child had drawn it, especially with the ridiculous trees. No wonder the world did not sit up and notice. And so Tikal was left to the jungle once more.

It took the Guatemalan government another century to get their act together. They built an airstrip (now the main road next to the Tikal Tourist Centre) and invited eminent American archaeologists to map and excavate the ruins. Then, when someone did a better drawing of the main temple, they stuck a picture of it on the front of all their quetzal banknotes. And so, with interest finally building, UNESCO representatives visited; they nodded, prodded some statues and studied the maps before adding it to their list of World Heritage Sites.

George Lucas heard about Tikal, and arrived with a camera crew to film scenes for his *Star Wars* movie. When the movie was screened across the globe, people watched the segment where Tikal was in the background (representing Yavin, a rebel base) and scratched their heads, wondering where this place was and, if it existed, if they could they visit it. When they discovered it was in a secluded corner of Guatemala, they all bought mosquito repellent and plane tickets. These original tourists all had to find accommodation down in Flores and be bussed to the ruins the next day. Then some bright spark decided to build a hotel just outside the ruins' entrance. It was such a hit that two more were built, one of which was where I was right now.

6

A terrific screeching sound shook me from my slumber. In my sleep-numbed brain, it was a devil fighting a demon. Then it screeched again, shaking any residual notion that it might be a nightmare. I sat up and took stock. The terrible squeals sounded like they were coming from right outside my window. And there they were again: a raucous screech, a tumultuous rustle of branches and a blood-curdling growl. They were probably monkeys, I reckoned. Or children being taken by jaguars. Even though it was just after 4 a.m., I was fully awake now and I peered behind the curtain, careful to avoid contact with the dead-insect gauze, but there was nothing except blackness. But whatever had caused the sound had now fallen silent. Maybe they were staring right at me, wondering what I'd taste like. When the tropical call of a billion insects resumed, I closed the curtains and returned to bed.

I managed to find sleep again, but then, less than an hour later, another noise came: a terrible noise from the sky. The humid air of the tropics had unleashed a deluge that seemed concentrated on my roof. I reckoned the roof must be made of metal, because I'd never heard such a racket. It was like someone hammering on a drum kit with a pair of metal tongs. I pressed the pillow to my ears and shrieked myself to an uneasy stillness. And then, with no ceasing of the rain, I gave up and switched on the light.

Nothing.

The fan was not working either. So the back-up generator had stopped working sometime in the early hours. No wonder it was so warm. It was five-thirty in the morning and I felt about as refreshed as a man who had never been refreshed. After scrabbling about for the torch, I switched it on to find my clothes.

Once dressed, I sat on the edge of the bed and considered my options. I couldn't go outside: that much was evident – not with jaguars on the loose. Besides, the tropical downpour would soak me in half a second. Neither could I go back to sleep: it would be like sleeping inside a cement mixer. In the end, I used a combination of torch light and phone light to read every page of my Tikal guide book again. Then, when the first stirrings of daylight appeared behind the curtains, I looked outside. Ignoring the hideous dead critters staring at me from their mesh cemetery, I appraised the weather.

Thick leaves and large red flowers were dripping with spilling rain. A waterfall cascaded from a banana tree and below it was a pond of moving concentric circles. Beyond the flowers, less than ten feet away was thick, twisting vegetation. The Jaguar Inn's website was indeed correct: the owners had built it in the middle of the jungle. If a jaguar had sloped by at that moment I should not have been surprised.

By eight a.m., the rain began to ease, which was good news because I needed to venture out to the reception building. After grabbing my hat, camera and mosquito repellent, I was in the rain, almost slipping on the slick pathway that led to the meeting area. After a quick cup of coffee and a slice of toast, I turned to see a squat, firm man in his late forties approaching my table. His name was Jose and, as well as possessing a friendly face, he was my Tikal guide for the next four hours.

"They were probably spider monkeys," said Jose in excellent English. I'd just told him about the scary screeches that had woken me up. "There are many of them in the jungle." He looked outside the reception building and assessed the weather. "It is forecast to clear up, but I think we should begin the tour now because we will beat all the tourists who are driving up from Flores."

I agreed and stood up. After I had donned my hat, I followed Jose to the exit of the Jaguar Inn. Outside, we immediately got drenched, but the dampness was tempered by the rising temperature, so it was actually a nice combination. Jose was in front, leading the way along a trail that led past the empty car park, trinket shops and the visitors' centre. The stalls were open, wares laid out on tables or hanging from walls. A man jumped as we approached. Ignoring the fridge magnets, Tikal T-shirts and painted cups, we each bought large bottles of water. That done, we set off towards the actual entrance of the ruins, walking along the old airstrip that was no longer there.

"Is it hard to become a Tikal guide?" I asked Jose.

"For some people, yes. They find it hard to learn English and learn all the facts. But when I became a guide thirty years ago, I was living in Guatemala City, where it was easier. I could already speak English and I learned the facts at college, but I went one step further and moved to Flores to do more research. I visited the ruins every day until I knew everything about them. Then I sat the exams to be a Tikal guide – which were easier in those days – and became a tour guide. Thirty years later, here I am." Jose paused. "I say thirty years, but I had a decade in the middle when I was a lecturer at the University of Guatemala. I have a Masters in archaeology. But the money was not too good, so I returned to being a regular tour guide."

Just beyond the stalls was the entrance to the ruins. None of the ruins were visible, just a panorama of thick, primeval jungle bisected by a small trail. After showing my entrance ticket to a bleary-eyed security official, we entered the jungle, where Jose stopped and pointed to a lofty tree that had no branches along its smooth white trunk until the very top, where it suddenly sprouted thick curling foliage. It looked like someone had stuck a few shrubs on top of a telegraph pole. "This is a sabre tree," Jose said. "It is the national tree of Guatemala. The Maya thought these trees linked the underworld to the sky. Even now, if people are in a forest chopping trees down, they will leave the sabre tree alone."

I felt the need to study the tree further and so walked up to its mighty trunk, shaking raindrops from my hat. From a distance, it had looked stark and plain, but up close, the trunk had row upon row of small cone-shaped thorns. They resembled shark's teeth. Some were sharp enough to pierce a man's stomach should he decide to hug it. Anyone who attempted to climb the white monster would be lacerated to death. I asked why the tree needed such protection.

"They stop water loss, and they also protect against animals."

I nodded, trying to picture a type of animal that wanted to get its chops around a thick tree trunk like this. Even without the thorns it would be a difficult munch. All I could come up with was an elephant, but they didn't live in Central America. And while I pondered this, Jose and I left the sabre tree and began a walk through a dense clump of trees (of every description) where the canopy above us was so thick that it began to block the sunlight and rain. In semi-darkness, Jose stooped down and picked up a small greenish-brown fruit about the size of a plum. The fruit was already open, revealing two halves of beige mush crawling with tiny ants.

"Smell it," offered Jose, presenting the fruit to my face.

I scrunched my face but did so, detecting a faintly sweet odour.

"The tree that this fruit comes from makes a natural chewing gum called chicle." He walked to a nearby tree that did not look different to any other. "When the Maya discovered that gum came from this tree, they used it to keep their teeth clean and to keep hunger at bay. In the 1860s, American chewing gum manufactures like Wrigley's came here and started using it in their products. Chicle collectors would cut small lines in the trunk and the gum would drip into their collection bags. But a century later, someone invented a synthetic gum and the companies left. The Guatemalan government had to pay a lot of money to the chicle farmers because of this. They were all starving."

Ten minutes later, Jose and I came to a large plastic-covered information sign that showed a photo of a jaguar. The cat looked powerful and dangerous. I asked whether he had seen one.

Jose nodded. "Twice."

I shot him a glance. "You did? Where? Not here?"

"Both were early in the morning, just before sunset. The first one was far away from here, and I only saw it for a second. The second jaguar was here in Tikal and I saw it for longer. I was walking with an Australian tourist and we saw the jaguar walking between two isolated temples. It was about one hundred metres away from us. The jaguar must have heard us because it stopped and looked at us. My heart stopped."

"Jesus! What did you do?"

"We stood still – that is the best thing to do if caught in the open by a jaguar – and then, thank God, it started walking again and disappeared into the jungle. But I remember we stayed still for maybe another two minutes, scanning the trees and listening to the sounds. And that was another thing: everything was silent – no birds, no monkeys, just very unnerving silence. Anyway, after a few more seconds of total stillness, we turned around and walked back the way we came."

I whistled in appreciation of the tale. "If I'd been there, I don't think I could've waited. I'm pretty sure I would've run as soon as I saw it."

"Then you would have probably died. Almost all the animals that a jaguar hunts try to run away. So, if you ran, it may have believed you were its prey."

I gestured to the jungle around us. "So could be jaguars in there, right now?"

Jose shrugged. "Maybe."

I spun my neck trying to spot jaguars.

"But I don't think you should worry; no one has ever been attacked by a jaguar in Tikal. These cats are too clever to deal with humans. They prefer to attack cattle. Come on, let's go and see some temples."

8

Because it was still early, Jose and I had Tikal to ourselves, which was great, apart from the fact that all I could now think about was jaguars. They probably preferred these quieter moments from which to mount their surprise attack, I reasoned. And another thing: just because a tourist had never been killed by one at Tikal, it didn't mean it couldn't happen. At least I'd make the news; my wife might even be proud. *British Tourist Fights with Jaguar and is Eaten.*

As I followed Jose along the trails, I kept a wary eye out, but thankfully the only wildlife I saw was a massive grasshopper and some noisy birds in the treetops. But then, ominously, another sound cut through the bird chatter, a deep-throated monster sound. Jose identified it as a howler monkey.

"Normally, you don't hear them at this time," he said. "They usually howl just before sunrise. Maybe something has startled them: perhaps a jaguar."

I did a sharp intake of breath.

"I'm only messing with you, Jason. But it is a good job you're wearing a hat today. Howler monkeys like to defecate on people. They sit in the branches and sometimes howl so hard that they poop out. I'm not joking."

We left the thick patch of forest and emerged into an open area of Tikal ruins: my first sighting. Jose waited for me take it all in: the old crumbling limestone walls blackened with tropical grime, the steps covered in green lichen and, through a clump of trees, the top section of a distant Maya pyramid. The scene looked like something out of an Indiana Jones film, especially with no one else there to witness it apart from us. The rain had almost stopped too, leaving the jungle to sizzle and steam for effect.

We climbed some steps which, Jose explained, were actually rows of stone seats, and then began a precarious walk along a high ledge. Below was a scene of pure Maya majesty: a large central plaza flanked by two enormous pyramids at each end. When people think of Tikal, or see a postcard of it, it is one of these two temples they see. I stood on the edge, risking life-threatening injuries, just to gawp at them.

Temple I, also known as the Temple of the Great Jaguar, looked in fine condition, reminding me of a giant stone Dalek. Unlike the pyramids of Egypt, it was smaller and thinner, but no less impressive, with a steep staircase leading from the ground to a door at the top. The doorway was covered in a metal fence, which Jose explained was to deter people from climbing up to look inside.

"Why? What's in there?"

"Nothing. But it used to be the Maya priests' chamber and is therefore sacred."

I ask Jose whether the people of modern-day Guatemala bore any physical resemblance to the Maya people who had lived in Tikal.

"If you look at me you are seeing what the Maya looked like. I'm not that tall – 5'6", like most Maya men. I have the same skin colour, the same eyes and the same hair colour. About fifty percent of the population in Guatemala share Maya DNA."

"So is that the same in Mexico, Honduras and the rest?"

"In the southern states of Mexico, like Yucatan, yes, but in Honduras, no. In Honduras, less than ten percent of the population are Maya; the rest are Mestizos: you know, mixed."

"So how did Guatemala keep such a large population?"

"Mainly because our country is very mountainous. The Spanish couldn't be bothered taking over every mountain village and so the Maya carried on with their lives."

We moved to a position that offered an obstruction-free view of everything below. I asked Jose whether he had even been to Honduras or El Salvador.

"I've never been to either. All I hear is how dangerous they are with their gangs. I've been to Panama, though. That's a nice place."

I took out my camera to take a photo of the Temple of the Jaguar, but Jose stopped me. "I think it wise you step back a little. I don't want you to fall. That's exactly what happened to a couple of tourists a few years ago on one of the temples. They were not watching where they were going and both fell to their deaths. From what I understand, their bones were sticking out of their skin at all sorts of unusual angles."

I moved back, took a photo and then followed Jose to ground level, keeping my wits about me as we negotiated the wet stepping stones back down. At the bottom, I regarded the Dalek step pyramid in front of me: the funeral shrine of Jasaw Chan K'awiil I, who presided over Tikal between the years 682 and 734, a period of time when the Maya settlement went through a great renaissance. When he died, aged about fifty (no one really knows when he was born to ascertain a more accurate age of his death), his body was interred within the great pyramid where it remained until 1962. That was the year archaeologists armed with tiny spades and special devices found his tomb. Jasaw Chan K'awiil's body, they discovered, had been placed on a carefully-woven mat, which in turn had been laid on a wooden bench. His skeleton was covered with jade, pearls and exquisitely-painted pots. Around this pile lay jaguar skins, human bones and a large beaded necklace that, when heaved onto a weighing scale, tipped out at four kilograms, the same as an adult cat.

"In the North Acropolis there is another tomb," Jose told me, "where archaeologists found the skeletons of nine sacrificial victims, all teenagers and young adults. They were arranged around the remains of a ruler called Yax Nuun Ayiin, put there to keep him company during the afterlife."

I considered this. "Were they his children?"

"Almost certainly not."

"How were they killed? They weren't buried alive, were they?"

"No. They were sacrificed by the priests. And they probably went into the tomb willingly."

While I pondered the terrible notion of young men and women offering themselves to be killed so that they could be interred with a king, I went off to climb Temple II, the funeral shrine of Jasaw Chan K'awil's wife.

9

Temple II is thirty-feet lower than Temple I. Like its counterpart, it is roughly the same shape, with a distinctive top section where Maya priests had once assembled for prayers and sacrifice. At the half-way point is a platform where tourists can, if they get up early enough, gather to watch the sunrise. Instead of having to scale the dangerous steps at the front, there was a wooden staircase around the back, which I found myself climbing. By the time I reached the viewing platform, I was panting like a jaguar about to feast on a human skull, but sucked in my raspy breathing when I saw a few other people, all of them young backpacker types, arriving behind me. I nodded at one young man sporting a ponytail and a healthy tan; he returned the gesture but then moved to look down at the ruins.

I joined him, keeping a discreet distance. Temple 1 was directly opposite, looking even more Dalek-like, and to my right and left were other important buildings of the complex, such as the Central and North Acropolis. These massive structures once housed the residential dwellings of the Tikal ruling class, with schools and administrative buildings taking up the rest of the space. If I strained my eyes, I could just about make out Jose chatting to a trinket seller he knew. Overhead, trees full of chirping birds and chattering insects provided a pleasing jungle orchestra. Tikal was, for my first flavour of Maya culture, a tasty treat.

At ground level, I found Jose and we continued our walk, meandering through dense jungle until we arrived at another staircase. Where it led was a mystery and Jose suggested I climb it, promising me an even better view if I undertook the arduous ascent.

"How arduous?"

"Not very."

"But still arduous?"

"For me, yes, but for you, a man in good fitness, it will be fine."

I nodded, flexed my flabby chest and began another climb of heavy breathing mixed with rapid heartbeats. At the half-way point, I could actually hear blood pumping through my ears but pushed on, especially as young children were running past me, racing ahead of their parents. When I reached the top to plant my flag, I found myself on another temple platform, this one the busiest so far. About fifty people were sitting on some steps staring out at an expanse of prime green jungle. In Tikal, there were no such things as safety fences; if anyone got too close to the lip of the platform and slipped, death would swiftly follow.

I kept well back from the edge, nodding at the scene ahead, the same one George Lucas had used in Star Wars. I could understand why Lucas had picked the spot: it was a primeval panorama of emerald stretching from left to right, broken only by the curious top sections of some Tikal temples. Hover a spaceship above the canopy and it would be an alien planet from a different solar system.

A boy aged about seven galloped from the staircase and ran across the front of the viewing platform with centimetres to spare. If he had slipped or if anyone had bumped him, he would have gone down. His mother evidently thought the same thing because, when she caught up with him, she walloped him hard across the head. He yelped and looked contrite enough for his mother to loosen her angry look. Even so, she made him sit down, which he did like a whipped dog.

Later, walking along a forest trail with Jose, I caught sight of quick movement – something shadowy flitting through dense roots and tree litter. And there it was again: definite animal movement. It was too small to be a jaguar, but it worried me nonetheless. "Did you see that?" I asked Jose.

"See what?"

We both stopped and appraised the jungle. And then the jungle beast appeared, except it was not one beast but several. At first I thought they were cats or perhaps thin-snouted monkeys.

"Coatis," said Jose. "A troop of females and young males."

There must have been about twenty of the racoon-like creatures, each with a cute head and lengthy tail. While we watched, the coatis crossed the trail and entered the jungle on the other side, where they began a snuffling competition. All of the mammals had their snouts in the forest litter, their paws digging through dead leaves and jungle grime until, occasionally, one would come up with a mouthful of jungle critter. One of their favourite titbits was tarantula.

"So where are the older males?" I asked.

"The mature males live by themselves. They fight too much to live with the main pack. But they will occasionally find the troop so they can mate. Then they go back to the jungle alone." Then, as quickly as they came, the coatis were gone, rustling through the undergrowth. Another distraction, though, was a pair of hooting toucans clattering about at the top of a tree. I'd never seen a toucan before and I was amazed by the size of their bills. They looked like curving, lopsided lollipops, all in yellow, green and orange. How they kept their balance was beyond my comprehension. But, according to Jose, a toucan's bill was actually very light, made of bone struts filled with a spongy material.

"But why have such large bills? Do they fight with them or something?"

"No, it keeps them cool. It's like an elephant's ears: the large surface area helps to cool the body."

We moved on through the jungle, and came to the Plaza of the Seven Temples. It was not in the same league as the Great Plaza, but worthy of a short stop. The name came from the seven small temples that edged the square, all in some sort of disrepair and, to be honest, not that much to look at. Even so, Jose gave a commentary about them, telling me about how the ground sloped towards the north east to help with the drainage of rainwater when, suddenly, he stopped talking. "Watch out: a snake!" Jose held out his arm to prevent me moving forward. We were standing in a small grassy area in the middle of the ruins.

"Where?" I was scanning the ground.

"In the grass. It's stopped moving and has its head in the air."

I studied the patch of grass where Jose was pointing but still could not see it. "What colour is it?"

"Green."

And then I spotted it: a beautiful snake, about four feet long, with striking black zigzags along the length of its body. Like Jose had said, its head was up in the air, a thin pink tongue flickering in and out as it tasted the air. I moved closer to take a photo.

"Be careful, Jason. It is a Mexican parrot snake. They get angry very quickly."

I stopped in my tracks. "Are they venomous?"

"Very mild venom, but painful bite."

"Do they eat Mexican parrots?"

"I'm not sure."

I moved with caution; I had no wish to receive a snake bite, even if it would not kill me. As I moved closer, its head swivelled in my direction, and then – as quick as a flash – it began charging. I fled and shrieked. The last time I'd shrieked like this had been in Indonesia. A few months previously, my wife and I had come across a large praying mantis sitting in the stairwell of the hotel where we had been staying. As I leaned in close, taking a video of the insect, it began to sway its head from side to side: a warning to back off. With my wife telling me to leave it alone, I zoomed in even closer and, suddenly, it flew up at my face, making me shriek and flee. My wife shrieked too because, as it flew past me by a millimetre, it headed towards her before flying over the side of the stairs. Back in Tikal, when I'd retreated to what I judged a safe distance, I turned to see Jose laughing. "It has gone, Jason. You can come back now."

After the snake incident, we proceeded with more caution, and then arrived into yet another wide plaza edged with jungle. It was time to say goodbye to Jose. He told me I had two options to get back to the Jaguar Lodge: the long way or the scenic short way. I looked at my watch. It was almost lunchtime; I'd been looking at the ruins for close to four hours. I decided the scenic short way was the option for me and so I headed to the trail that would take me along it, watching Jose bound off towards another guide who looked like he had had just finished his morning tour.

A few minutes later, only several hundred metres into my walk, I began to feel decidedly uneasy. Here I was, a lone person walking along a lonely jungle trail where big cats lived. And why wasn't anyone else walking the trail? Jose had said the trail was about a kilometre in length, a fifteen to twenty minute walk, but he didn't mention it would be through hostile jaguar territory.

I scanned the jungle for signs of eyes, but realised this was a bad idea. If a jaguar was coming, I'd rather not know. A quick bite to the back of my neck, and that would be the end. The thought of this made me quicken my pace, fearful now of every dark shadow and bush rustle. How unlucky it would be, I thought, to be the first person eaten by a jaguar in Tikal since records began. That was if my body was ever found. The insects didn't help matters, either; every now and again they would fall silent, making it easy to think a jaguar was nearby. And then, before I could break into a panicked, arm-flailing run, I spied the finish line. Five minutes later, I was safely ensconced inside the Jaguar Inn.

10

Xavier, the man who had delivered me to Tikal, was driving me back to Flores Island. I would be staying the night there before my flight to San Salvador the next day.

"Tikal good?" Xavier asked.

I nodded. "Very good. Lots to see." I noticed we were approaching another of those yellow jaguar road signs I had seen the previous evening. I asked Xavier to stop so I could get a photo of me standing next to it. A minute later, I was at the sign, thinking of the irony of being dragged into the jungle by a jaguar next to a sign warning people about them. Back on the road, we passed the national park security gates and then slowed down because of a cowboy. He was riding a horse and pulling another horse behind him. Behind the second horse was a dog, all three connected by ropes. The dog was trotting along happily enough and, as we passed, the man in the cowboy hat smiled like a Maya Clint Eastwood.

I was looking forward to Isla de Flores, to wander its cobblestone lanes, to gaze at the red terracotta roofs and to maybe hire a boat to experience Guatemalan life from the lake. During Spanish colonial times, the tiny island had been the last Maya stronghold against European invaders, its location geographically advantageous to repelling the Spanish because of the water surrounding it. Plus it was so far inland that the Spanish had not thought to bring boats. So the Maya had battened down the hatches and, whenever the Spanish came too close, they fired arrows or blew darts through tubes to keep them at bay. The Spanish ransacked the mainland instead.

From the safety of Flores Island, the Maya learned that something terrible was unfolding across the water. Their brethren were succumbing to a deadly disease that covered their bodies in hideous smelling pustules that ended up rotting the skin until the person was dead. The disease was smallpox, imported by the Spanish. Then some Spanish boats and weapons arrived. The year was 1697 and the Maya of Flores Island knew their time was up. Unable to ward off such a force, they fled, disappearing into the jungles by boat, allowing the Spanish to destroy their prized central pyramid and burn down almost everything else.

Xavier and I hit the outskirts of Flores town, a settlement made up of three parts: the island of Flores, the town of San Benito and another town called Santa Elena. All three merged into one urban area. San Benito made headlines in 2011 when a horrifying massacre took place there. In a farm close to town, raiders armed with guns, machetes and knives killed twenty-seven people, all of them labourers. One victim was found with the letter Z carved into his stomach, a crude but effective reference to a notorious Mexican drug cartel called Los Zetas.

Los Zetas is regarded by the United States as the most sophisticated drug gang in Mexico. It began in the 1980s, when a group of disgruntled but highly-trained military personnel found more lucrative employment working as muscle men for drug cartels. In 2010, after three decades of watching and learning, they broke away and formed their own cartel, quickly establishing themselves as the most brutally efficient gang in operation, eclipsing all others with their level of orchestrated and systematic violence. The Los Zetas cartel is not a group to mess with, as the owner of the farm had found out.

As well as the man with a carved Z in his stomach, everyone had been decapitated, their heads left scattered across a field. One of the attackers had collected enough spilled blood to daub the front of the ranch with a message. It was a chilling warning to the farm owner that they were coming for him. The cartel had already killed the man's daughter, cutting her up into pieces as encouragement for him to hand over the drug shipment he had allegedly stolen.

The town of Flores was nondescript. Past the airport, it was the domain of a Pizza Hut, a petrol station, a collection of ramshackle shops (including one that specialised in aluminium products), a tiny shopping mall and plenty of people on small motorcycles. One woman had somehow squeezed herself and four children onto her moped, three sitting behind and one, a little boy aged about four, standing in the footwell in front. If a truck smashed into them, they wouldn't stand a chance. After clearing some traffic lights, we turned away from the town and drove across a short causeway towards the island.

Flores looked gorgeous. Even though the Spanish had destroyed almost all the Maya sites, they had constructed colonial beauty in their wake, all contained within the perimeter of a small island that could be walked around in less than twenty minutes. Though long past its best, with peeling paintwork, cracked pavements and an assorted collection of grime-coated buildings, Flores Island was the prettiest place on my travels thus far.

My place of stay, appropriately enough, was the Isla de Flores Hotel, and was supremely colonial. The room featured a wooden shuttered doorway that led onto a small balcony edged by a wrought iron fence. Below me, the people of Flores had hung their washing out to dry beside arched windows. Above me, pigeons cooed in the terracotta rafters. Beyond the buildings was the gorgeous, glinting lake. Instead of drug cartels robbing me, the Guatemalan badlands of Central America were wooing me with their sights and sounds

Outside, with the afternoon in full swing, I set off to explore the island. My hotel was along a cobblestone street guarded by a blue-uniformed policeman standing at the corner. When I passed, I nodded; he smiled in return, keeping one hand on the handle of his gun. Around the corner, the street led down towards the lake, lined on both sides by painted homes in pastel colours. Little red tuk-tuks rattled over the stones, their drivers occasionally beeping to attract my attention. Instead of walking downwards, I headed uphill. In the middle of island, at its highest point, was a twin bell towered cathedral in white. From a distance, it looked grand but up close, like many buildings in town, I could see the grime and peeling paint. Inside was interesting for its black Jesus Christ, one of only two in Guatemala, the colour the result of wood-staining rather than for any racial reasons.

I walked down to the lake, home to small pleasure craft, and their drivers waved for my attention. I mimed I was walking around the island, but would be back. I carried on with my loop around the western side of Flores Island, passing a small wooden cart selling corn on the cob. A pot-bellied old man standing near an equally old bicycle was eating one with audible zest. "Hola," he said between mouthfuls as I passed.

"Hola," I replied, walking on. When I stopped to admire the lake just along from him, the man came over to join me.

"Where you from, amigo?"

I told him.

He took a bite of his corn on the cob and nodded. "Not many people come here from your country. But I love people from England!"

I quickly found out that the man's name was Carlos and he worked in a hotel restaurant in the main part of town. After his shift, he always cycled to this same corn stand for an evening snack. Then he seemed to have an idea and rushed off to the vendor to buy another corn on the cob. Instead of keeping it for himself, he gave it to me.

"No, I couldn't..."

Carlos pressed it into my hand. "I insist. This is my gift to the people of England. When you go back home, you can tell everyone that Carlos loves them."

Wondering whether the man had drunk too many tequilas, I took the corn and bit into it. It really was delicious and, now that I'd had one bite, I suddenly wanted another. Three minutes later, it was finished and I thanked Carlos for his unbidden generosity.

"Enjoy Guatemala, amigo," he said as we parted ways. "We are not all drug runners and gang bangers."

Further into my circuit, I realised that Flores could have been a village in Spain or Italy. The buildings had that Mediterranean feel: the curves of the arches, the pretty little wooden balconies busy with flower pots and patterned stonework; even the people looked slightly Mediterranean, from the old woman in the flowery dress sitting on a wall with her husband to a couple of teenagers who danced the cobbles with mobile phones pressed against their ears. The cafés also added to the Mediterranean impression. One thing spoiling the effect was some of the roofing material choices. Instead of red terracotta, many had ugly corrugated metal sheets.

A couple of men walked toward me. One looked every inch the cartel drug lord: middle-aged, black but greying hair, thin moustache and steely gaze. With him was another man, probably his lieutenant. Both looked like they were packing heat. As we approached point zero, I decided to smile. "Hola," I chirped.

The men's expressions changed immediately. Both morphed from crazed Mafiosi to friendly locals in less than half a second. "Hola, amigo," Boss Man said as we all passed.

At the northern tip of Flores I found more hotels and restaurants, including one called Big Tacos, and then, just seventeen minutes after setting off, I found I had done the complete circle. It was now time for a boat ride.

12

The boat commander, a thick-set man in his late twenties wearing a blue T-shirt and white cap, appraised me. "For one hour, the price is three hundred quetzals."

I mentally calculated this. It wasn't difficult because three hundred quetzals corresponded to thirty pounds. "How about seventy-five for half an hour?"

I expected the man to argue the toss but he capitulated straight away and so I climbed into his narrow vessel, which was painted the same colour as his T-shirt. A few seconds later, we powered away from dry land, heading across the lake towards an even tinier island than Flores. With the soothing breeze now caressing my brow, I sat back and relaxed. Boat trips were always a highlight of any trip.

The island was home to a tiny museum, which was closed. Instead, there was an enormous lizard to look at. It was resting on a thick bank of branches, scrutinising us as we approached from the water. It looked like a dinosaur with spines all the way down its back.

"That is a green iguana," said the boatman. "Notice the two horns on its snout. Only iguanas from Guatemala and Mexico have them."

I looked at the horns; they looked like two mini rhinoceros horns. Then I regarded the rest of the lizard's body. It was about four feet in length and more beige than green. If it was provoked, its set of sharp teeth could shred the skin off a person's hand. I was thankful it ate only plants. "How did it get on the island?" I asked

"Swam. They are good swimmers."

"Do people eat them here?" I'd read that in Nicaragua, during a recent drought when the price of chicken had risen dramatically, people took to eating iguanas because they tasted like chicken and people could catch the lizards at the bottom of their gardens. The government even encouraged this behaviour.

"Of course. But it's not very common. I have eaten lizard meat a few times. But I'll tell you something: if you did not know it was lizard, you would think it was chicken."

On our way again, I questioned the boatman about hurricanes. He nodded straight away. "There was a big one last August: Hurricane Earl. It came about three in the morning. All the electricity went off and you should've heard the wind and rain! When the sun came up, I looked outside and saw rain going horizontally. And you know when you see hurricanes on TV – with the palm trees all blowing sideways? Well, that's exactly what it was like. Of course, many roofs had blown away."

"So that's why there are all those corrugated metal roofs in town?"

"Right."

Beyond the island, on the other side of the lake, was a line of pretty buildings set into the hills. Each featured wide verandas and vibrantly painted walls. One had something strange in the garden, though. It was a ten-foot tall papier-mâché woman wearing a frilly pink dress. Her face was rudimentary, as if a primary school class had made it.

"She is for the Dance of the Chotona, the dance of the dolls," the boatman informed me. "At the start of spring, all over town you will see these dolls. Each is large enough for a person to fit inside. People parade around the streets in them while everyone else sings and dances. Firecrackers go off everywhere. It's a very famous festival here."

I tried to picture the scene: masses of people prancing around the tight cobbles of Flores while fireworks ricocheted against hotel windows. "Why the giant woman, though?"

"I'm not too sure, but I think many years ago there was a tall woman who helped us fight against Mexico. She died when a snake bit her or something. But it doesn't matter who she was; the Dance of the Chotona is just a good time to have a party. If you get chance, you should come back to Flores and see it."

The other side of the lake also had a statue of a horse in full gallop. A cat was sitting in the shade underneath the horse; behind it sat a man reading a newspaper and another man with a toddler in his lap. When Spanish conquistador Herman Cortes visited the area in the mid sixteenth century, he was so drained from fighting his way through the jungle that he didn't bother fighting the local Maya tribe and instead made friends with them. He did not linger, though but, as a gift to the local chieftain he left behind a lame horse with an injured ankle. The locals had never seen a horse before; instead of eating it, they tried to nurse it back to health by feeding it flowers and a strange chicken broth they liked to eat. But the horse didn't like the strange medicine and, after neighing its last breath, it promptly died. The people of Flores stared at the dead horse and scratched their heads. Then someone suggested they bury it and make a statue in its likeness, which is what happened. Over time, people forgot why they had made the statue and began praying to it instead. When the Spanish returned seventy-five years later and witnessed the local people worshipping the horse statue as a god, they smashed it to pieces.

After traversing the underside of the causeway, we were back where we started. I thanked the boatman, paid him a nice tip and bounded ashore. It was early evening and the townsfolk of Flores Island were sitting on the wall that surrounded the western edge of the island. Most were enjoying deep conversation as they scoffed down burritos and corn. The whole town was out it seemed and the tuk-tuks were having a hard time getting around the swell of people.

As for me, I headed back to the hotel and, later that evening, as night descended over Guatemala, I sipped on a couple of Gallo beers, thinking about how much the country had offered me in such a short time. As well as the Tikal ruins and the island of Flores, Guatemala's greatest gift was its people. Guatemalans were some of the friendliest folk I had met on my travels, often going out of their way to smile or nod at me. But, speaking of misunderstood nations, the next day I would be visiting one of the most notorious nations of Central America: El Salvador. When I told people back home of my plans to head there, most had whistled or taken sharp intakes of breath. The general consensus was that I should not be visiting El Salvador, a country with a proliferation of gangs. But was El Salvador, like Guatemala, misunderstood by the world at large, or did it warrant its many warnings? The next day I should find out.

TIKAL/FLORES
Top: Isla de Flores from aboard a Tropic Air Cessna; Temple 1, Tikal; Me
risking my life to pose in prime jaguar country
Middle: Steep streets abound on Flores island; A Mexican parrot snake; One
of the giant models used in the Dance of the Dolls festival
Bottom: A green iguana – note the horns on its snout; Flores as seen from my
boat ride

Chapter 4. San Salvador, El Salvador

FCO Advice: Violence between gangs is a growing problem. Take particular care in downtown San Salvador. Foreigners have been targeted when leaving the airport. There remains a small risk of kidnapping.

My connecting flight to Guatemala City left dead on time and we were soon flying over thick jungle. Then, before I knew it, we began descending. In the distance, a brooding series of volcanic peaks, all beautifully bathed in morning sunshine, signalled we were close to Guatemala City. I looked down and there it was: a sprawling city of over thirteen million, the most populous urban area in Central America.

Tightly-packed, low-rise slums stretched across verdant hills with little forethought for zonal planning. Down in these straggly districts, Guatemalan gangs fought the daily battle to control the extortion rackets, prostitution rings and arms trafficking routes. I'd read that in some shanties of Guatemala City, virtually every schoolchild knew of someone killed as a result of this gang violence. Fuelled by a lack of family cohesion and rampant poverty, teenage boys (and sometimes girls) joined the lower ranks to receive a smidgeon of the misguided respect that membership of a gang offered. In a country where serious violence is seen as the norm rather than the extreme, these teenagers find their niche.

One sickening incident of violence I heard about involved a teenage girl. In May 2015, a vigilante mob surrounded the girl, then punched and kicked her until she was on the ground. Then they poured petrol over her. While someone filmed the attack, a member of the mob threw a match. In flames, the girl rolled around, desperately screaming for help while the mob jeered. No-one offered any assistance. When the girl was dead, the crowd, which included young children and the elderly, departed. Later, when asked why they had murdered the teenage girl, the vigilantes claimed that she was part of a gang that had robbed and killed a 68-year-old taxi driver, one of their friends.

And the truly upsetting thing about this terrible case is that the police have never identified the girl. And neither have they charged anyone for her murder. She is just another statistic in a series of grim homicides across Guatemala. According to the latest figures, there are over one hundred people murdered in Guatemala City every week, and only four of each week's killings will be solved. I would learn more about gang violence when I got to El Salvador, but for now, I looked down upon areas of prime crime until they were replaced by the gated residential communities of the rich. Towards its centre, Guatemala City looked about as affluent as anywhere else, with skyscrapers, highways and pretty patches of green lining its wide boulevards. It all formed a formidable barrier that kept the poor out.

2

As our Avianca turboprop taxied to the gate, I noticed a white executive jet parked on the apron. Judging by the orange engine covers and dirty streaks along its fuselage and wings, the plane had not flown in a long time. I hypothesised that it might have belonged to a captured drug dealer before it was impounded. Or maybe Mr Big abandoned it so he could escape across the border to Honduras. In reality, it was probably nothing to do with either of those scenarios, but it did make me think. Huge amounts of cocaine (around 400 tons annually) pour in from Honduras on their way to Mexico and then the United States. With a street value of over thirty billion dollars, this is more than the GDP of half the countries in the world. And Guatemala's long unpoliced coastlines, together with its proliferation of hidden jungle airstrips, are to blame, making the nation the ideal stopover for the transhipment of drugs. And because many of their interests lie on Guatemalan soil, Mexican cartels have moved into the border areas to control the shipments. Some of them have branched out with poppy plantations in order to expedite the manufacture and sale of heroin, a big money spinner for them in the towns and cities of the United States.

After grabbing my bag, I headed into the domestic arrivals terminal of the airport. I needed to get to international departures and so attempted to cross, becoming utterly lost in the process. As far as I could tell, there were no signs telling me where to go and, whenever I stopped to ask someone, the look of incomprehension on their faces told me I was on my own. After twenty minutes of aimless wandering and backtracking, I gave up and stepped outside into the sunshine and heat. I spied a policeman and asked for help. He shook his head and shrugged.

In all my travels, in all the countless airports I had travelled through, Guatemala's La Aurora Airport was proving the most bothersome. In the end, I found a line of taxis and asked a driver to take me to international departures. He looked as confused as the policeman, but summoned a dispatcher who ended up being my saviour. After hearing my sorry plight, he led me into a building opposite where he pointed out a derelict-looking elevator. Without his assistance, I would never have found it. I was so thankful, I gave him fifty quetzals as a reward.

But there was good news waiting for me at the check-in desk. For some reason, Avianca had upgraded me to business class, which meant my seat was the quite luxurious 1A. For the thirty-minute flight to San Salvador, I nibbled on a plate of nuts and sipped on a glass of champagne, staring outside at a long sandy coastline so straight that it looked like it had been drawn with a ruler. As we came in to land, patchworks of agricultural fields came into view. All had huge buildings in their centre, most with swimming pools. Did farmers have swimming pools, I wondered? Maybe they did. Or were these the homes of Salvadoran drug barons? I had no time to ponder, because we were soon on the runway. I had arrived in the danger zone of El Salvador.

3

El Salvador was the edgiest country of my trip. The mention of its name sends shivers down the spines of all but the most intrepid of tourists. To me, El Salvador conjured images of drug lords living in graffiti-covered compounds, surrounded by their tattooed lieutenants and spent bullet casings. Outside their heavily-guarded blocks, street corners bristled with young men lounging on walls with handguns tucked into their shirts. The picture was not inviting in the least, yet I was intrigued. I didn't know anyone who had been to El Salvador, and that was a magnet to me. But coming in at number one in world murder rankings, El Salvador was the most likely place I'd be a victim of crime.

Gangs play a huge part in the negative press El Salvador receives, as does the dreadful civil war, the memories of which still linger. The Salvadoran Civil War lasted from 1979 until 1992, causing millions to flee El Salvador into neighbouring countries or the US. During the conflict, death squads patrolled the nation's cities, instilling fear and causing the disappearance of thousands. They were also responsible for a series of state-sanctioned massacres, the worst of which was the El Mozote Massacre.

El Mozote was a village up near the Honduras border, home to around eight hundred people. In December 1981, a troop of government soldiers calling themselves the Angels of Hell arrived there to flush out some anti-government guerrillas. After dragging people from their homes, the soldiers ordered everyone to lie down in the middle of the village plaza. There, the villagers were offered a stark choice: give up the hiding places of the guerrillas and live, or keep quiet and die. There was a problem with this, though: the people of El Mozote had no idea where the guerrillas were hiding and so they had no choice but to take option two. To jog non-existent memories, the Angels of Hell kicked and stamped on a few heads. When no information was forthcoming, they told everyone to return to their homes. If anyone dared to set foot outside, the soldiers told them, they would be shot. And so, with the town eerily quiet, the soldiers planned their next move.

Early the next morning, everyone was ordered back into the central square again. The villagers were split into two groups: male and female. Again, they were given the chance to reveal the whereabouts of the guerrillas. When no one offered any information, the commander nodded and gave the order to commence with the plan. While some of his soldiers herded the two hundred or so men and older boys into the town's small church, the women and older girls were marched up onto the hillside that overlooked the village. As for the small children and babies, they were locked up inside a few houses in the village centre.

Inside the church, ordinarily a place of worship, the soldiers asked the men to give up the hiding places of the guerrillas. No one spoke and so a few villagers were singled out. At the front of the church, in full view of their friends and neighbours, the men were held down and their tongues were cut off. The soldiers asked the rest of the group whether they wanted to say anything now. When no one stepped forward, the Angels of Hell started dislocating the men's limbs and gouging out their eyes. Then they brought out the machetes. The women on the hill could hear the men's screams.

Imagine how it must have been for the men in that church to watch their own kin being tortured and mutilated, knowing they could do nothing about it and that they were next. They could have lied, one supposes, but that would have been a risky venture. What if the soldiers discovered the lie? What if some soldiers stayed in the village while the others went off to search for non-existent guerrillas? What if they didn't believe them anyway? So the men kept quiet as their friends at the front were hacked to death.

At the same time the men were being brutalised, the women and girls on the hill were being raped, murdered and then set on fire. After finishing with them, the soldiers climbed down the hill and entered the houses. In the next few horrible minutes, they killed every baby and child. In some cases, they simply set fire to houses to let them burn to death.

Back in the church, with carnage going on outside, the Angels of Hell told the men it was their final chance to give up the information they needed. No one spoke. So this was it, then: the final scene in the terrible play. Every one of the assembled men and teenagers was either decapitated or shot dead.

After killing every man, women and child, the soldiers killed all the town's animals before setting fire to everything. They did not want to leave any evidence of the crimes they had committed. With the village alight, everyone lay dead, half of them children. And that would have been that, except for one small detail.

Someone was still alive.

A 38-year-old village woman called Rufina Amaya had watched it all from her hiding place. When the village women had been marched up the hill earlier, she had found herself at the back of the line. This placement meant that, when the group rounded a bend, she managed to slip away unnoticed. From her hidden vantage point in a tree, she heard the screams and gunshots from the church. At one point, she saw a soldier drag a man from the church and decapitate him. The man was her husband. How she had the presence of mind not to break cover is a mystery, but Rufina Amaya held her nerve, even when she saw soldiers set fire to the house inside of which were her children. At one point, according to the testimony she later gave, Rufina saw her nine-year-old son run out of the house screaming. He was soon silenced with a shot to the head.

Rufina remained hidden all night. The next morning, after watching the soldiers depart, she made a run for it and fled through the countryside. She eventually made it to the Honduran border, where she became a refugee. When her story surfaced a few weeks later, world condemnation was instant and leaders across all continents wanted answers. The Salvadorian government vehemently denied that civilians had been targeted, saying that those killed were guerrillas or guerrilla sympathisers. Eventually, though, with testimony from Rufina Amaya and exhumed bodies of children with bullets holes through their skulls, they could deny it no longer. Despite this, the men who committed the atrocities were never brought to justice, their identities hidden under amnesty laws and a supposed lack of army records. As for Rufina Amaya, she eventually remarried and had more children. In her later years she moved back to San Salvador where she finally died in 2007, aged 64. The village of El Mozote lives on too, with a few scattered houses, a new church and a memorial to those who lost their lives in two terrible days.

4

"Welcome to El Salvador; my name is Edgar," grinned a stocky man in his late thirties. Edgar possessed an enviable shock of black hair, and his friendly face made me warm to him straight away, which was great since he was going to be my guide for the next few days. "Is this your first time here?" His accent was thick but perfectly understandable.

I nodded.

"It's good that tourists are starting to come. This is what the government wants and what I want." He led me outside into the blinkingly bright sunshine. "Wait here, I'll get the car. I should only be a couple of minutes."

With that he was gone, leaving me alone to take in this most dangerous of Central American cities. I kept my back to the wall and surveyed the vicinity. To my left were rows of luggage trolleys. As I watched, a woman got one and walked off with her young daughter. Across from me, some airport workers were eating their lunches from sandwich boxes. To my right was a line of parked cars. Everyone looked perfectly normal and law-abiding. So far, so good.

On the road to the city centre, things looked good, too. The road was well paved and the palms were adding a nice touch of the tropics. Roadside stalls were selling piles of fruit and vegetables, and behind them, all-purpose convenience stores peddled mops, brooms and jugs. In a small café, emblazoned with a huge Pepsi logo, three white-aproned women sat waiting for customers. For a city under the cosh of crime gangs, things looked remarkably normal. I decided to ask Edgar what he liked about El Salvador.

He thought for a moment. We were passing a long green-and-yellow chicken bus. It was in the far right lane, bound for a place called San Marcos, a small town southeast of the capital. We passed it and headed straight on, towards San Salvador. "Good question…I can think of two things straight away: the heritage of my country, as we have some fine colonial buildings, and second, the wildlife. The number of birds we have in El Salvador is staggering. Are you interested in birds?"

I shrugged. "Not really."

"I am. I love birds. The third thing is … the scenery. We have volcanoes, jungles, great coastal areas. El Salvador can easily compete with Costa Rica and Belize if we get things right."

I asked him what he meant.

"Well the government can do much better for a start. Corruption is a concern. Money comes in, money disappears. Who loses out? Us! And the gangs are another problem. A big problem. So safety is a concern, but this is improving. It's one thing the government does right. Take this road we're on right now. Seven or eight years ago, I would not feel safe along here. Every day there were would have been carjackings or kidnappings. But now, none."

"Why is that?"

"The army. They shoot all the bad guys. This government call this policy *mano dura,* which means iron fist. And they mean just that. If the police or army think you're part of a gang, then bang, bang: you're dead. Fire first and ask questions later. The government is finally cleaning up our city. I think it's great."

Others might disagree. Earlier in the year, a troop of soldiers had cornered some teenagers in an alleyway. The boys had been on their way home after celebrating a friend's birthday. After the soldiers had told the boys to lie face down in the dirt, two of the teenagers made a run for it. The soldiers shot them dead. After subduing the other boys, the police started to clean up the mess until a van arrived and whisked them away. Another van arrived seconds later – the clean-up team. Officially, the killings were reported as gang violence, even though the mother of one of the dead boys claimed her son had never been part of a gang. It didn't matter; the case was closed and that was that. If a few stray civilians got caught up in the fight against gangs, then that was the price to pay for cleaning up the streets of the capital.

Even so, gang violence continues to blight El Salvador. I decided to broach the subject of gangs with Edgar.

He sighed and began to speak.

5

"There are two main gangs in my country," Edgar told me. "Mara Salvatrucha and Calle 18, often called MS-13 and the 18th Street Gang. They hate each other. If there's a murder in the city, almost always it will involve these gangs fighting each other. Between them, they have about 25,000 members, mainly young boys between 15 and 25. This is something that scares me. I have a nine-year-old son. His mother and I worry about him being caught up in the gangs. But at the moment, he wants to be a policeman. I think he likes the uniform."

Outside, a bright-orange chicken bus caught my eye. It looked great, far better than the straightforward yellow school bus it had started out as in the United States. It was passing a series of large homes covered in barbed wire and electric fencing. Sitting outside some of the dwellings were armed security guards. "Both these gangs," continued Edgar, "started in the United States."

Edgar explained that, during the El Salvador Civil War, thousands of Salvadorans fled the country and many had ended up in Los Angeles. "And when they got there, they had more important things to think about than making sure their kids did their homework or went to school, so by the time these boys were twelve or thirteen, they were out in the streets looking for trouble. And trouble always finds trouble. These boys, who hardly spoke English, gravitated to the Mexican kids who also wanted trouble. Soon they were in gangs."

I asked why Jose's family hadn't moved to America.

"My mother thought about going – she told me this years after – but she was a single parent with three kids; it was hard for her to move. So we stayed in El Salvador and grew up during the civil war." Jose looked wistful. "I remember seeing bits of paper stuck onto lampposts near where we lived. They were lists of people suspected as government informants. Where we lived, most people were against the government so I'd look at these lists and sometimes see a name I recognised – maybe a neighbour, maybe someone who worked in the local store – and I'd think, oh-oh, they're in trouble."

"What happened to them?"

"I don't know; I was only a kid. But I reckon they moved away pretty quickly if they knew their name was on the list. Being a government spy was a bad thing. I remember another time. I was around my friend's house watching TV on an old black-and-white portable. It was dark outside and we were catching *The Flintstones*. That sticks in my mind: The Flintstones! What a thing to remember, huh? Anyway, we were watching the TV when another of our friends rushes in through the door, switches off the TV and turns off the lights. He tells us to be quiet and not move. So we all sit there in the dark, wondering what's going on and then we see them: guerrillas. They were outside on the street, walking past the house; I was so scared, but excited at the same time. We knew about the guerrillas, of course, but usually they stayed up in the mountains; I'd never seen one before. And so we waited, still as mice, until they had gone. We must have sat there for two hours. By the time I got home, my mother was raving, asking where I'd been and why I'd been out so long. I told her I'd fallen asleep and didn't mention the guerrillas. I didn't want to upset her."

"What a memory."

"Yeah, but we were just kids growing up. To us, things like that just happened and then we forgot about them. Like when we'd hear the pot-pot-pot of guns at night. Sometimes there would be shots fired back. But my mother had the ten-minute rule. If the gunshots stopped before ten minutes, then we could carry on and go to sleep. But if they carried on past ten minutes, or sounded like they were getting really close, then we had to meet downstairs and be ready to run. Thankfully, it never happened, or, if it did, I don't remember. Anyway, we were talking about the gangs in Los Angeles, right?"

I waited for Jose to continue.

"So these Salvadoran boys joined the gangs and got the tattoos. They had the hot girls and all the money – all from illegal activities – and they thought they'd hit the big time. And that's how it was for a while: two large Salvadoran gangs living in Los Angeles. But then things changed in the mid-90s."

Jose told me that the US implemented a new policy whereby any foreign immigrant, once arrested and found guilty of a crime, had to be deported back to their home country. Soon, thousands of Salvadoran gang bangers were on their way back to El Salvador. "And when they got here, do you think they changed their ways? Of course not! These young guys wanted the same good life they had back in the States. They were earning a thousand dollars a month working for the cartels in LA, but the only work they could find here was washing dishes or picking bananas for a tenth of that. No, they did not accept this, and so the gangs reformed and then became our problem."

"Where does the name MS-13 come from?"

"Mara Salvtrucha is Salvadoran slang for a peasant guerrilla gang. The number 13 is how long a new member of the gang has to stand a beating from other gang members: thirteen seconds, which may not sound like long, but when you've got seven or eight guys kicking the shit out of you, it is."

Once accepted into a gang, Jose explained, the new recruit was expected to cover themselves in tattoos. They also learned a complicated series of hand signals so they could secretly communicate with one another. In the complex world of prostitution, racketeering, arms dealing, drug trafficking, extortion, money laundering and murder, they needed these secretive languages. In 2005, MS-13 was voted the most dangerous gang in the world; their rivals, the 18th Street Gang, came in at number two. In some ways they are worse because they have more members.

"About five years ago, the gangs called a truce. The murder rate dropped straight away. It lasted about three years. Since then, it's business as usual. What makes me laugh is some of the old guys. They are too old to do the gang stuff and so they leave. But they think that because they are not in the gang any more, they can go into parts of the city owned by the other gang. But the gangs have long memories. I keep reading about these old men crossing into a rival part of San Salvador and getting shot. That's why we need the iron fist policy. It's the only way to keep the gangs at bay."

6

Our first stop on our tour of San Salvador was a military museum. It was full of old armoured vehicles, tanks, aircraft and the like, most contained within the rear courtyard of a large white building. Flapping on the roof was a massive Salvadorian flag, featuring the standard blue and white horizontal layers. El Salvador's, Honduras' and Nicaragua's national flags were almost identical.

"Why so many guards?" I asked. Watching Edgar and me were couple of security officials wearing military fatigues and caps, and carrying large automatic weapons. "I thought this was a museum? Is it safe here?"

Edgar laughed. "This is nothing. Wait until we get to the city centre. But these men are here for reassurance. If I was a bad guy, I'd think twice about robbing you right now."

"So there might be bad guys outside the gates?"

Edgar shook his head. "There are no bad guys around here. Maybe after dark, there might be. But my point is that these guards are a deterrent, and a good one." He paused and looked around. "Listen, Jason. What can you hear?"

I tuned my ears into the surroundings. All I could hear were a few birds, a distant car engine and some strange bleats from a family of goats that were munching away on some nearby bushes. I told him this.

"Exactly. In the bad districts you'd hear the pop-pop-pop of gunshots. We won't be going to anywhere like that. I promise you."

The best feature of the museum was not any of its military history, but a massive topographical map. Just outside the entrance of the white building, down some steps, lay a mass of miniature sculpted volcanoes, lakes and rivers. San Salvador was nestled between some of the spiked green peaks. The city, a little sign told me, was 659 metres, or over two thousand feet above sea level. The volcano behind towered over six thousand feet above sea level.

"After we've seen the city centre," Edgar told me, "we will drive up that volcano. It's close to the city, as you can see. It's called the San Salvador Volcano."

"Is it safe?"

"You are asking that question a lot, my friend. But yes, it's safe. Its last eruption was a century ago. But I don't think it killed anyone. It just fizzed and steamed and some lava flowed down the sides. There were a few loud bangs, though, and people probably thought it was going to blow its top. It did make the old crater lake evaporate. But apart from that, nothing happened."

"So there was no damage to the city?"

"Oh yeah, there was damage. But it was from the earthquake before the eruption. But since then, the San Salvador Volcano has been sleeping."

7

As we threaded our way into the central core, I caught my first glimpse of the volcano. It was a classic cone shape and it looked like smoke was billowing out from the top. I pointed it out to Edgar.

"You worry too much. It's a cloud."

Downtown San Salvador was a busy hive of traffic jams and street stalls, but mostly there was building work. In fact it seemed as if the whole city was undergoing some sort of major reconstruction. Edgar slowed. "See that building there? The one lower than the others?" On my right was a structure covered in scaffolding. Edgar said, "It used to be a tall hotel before the earthquake of 1986. Thirty years later and they have finally decided to fix it."

The 1986 San Salvador earthquake was a bad one. Striking just before lunchtime, it shook the city to bits, demolishing countless buildings and causing deadly landslides. It killed over a thousand people. I asked Edgar whether he had been in the city at the time.

"Of course. I was nine years old. I can remember the day of the earthquake clearly. It was in October, just two days before my birthday. I was playing football with my friends when I heard what I thought was a large truck going by. *Whoosh!* it went. But there was no truck. Then the ground looked like a snake, all wavy, going up and down. I was surprised none of us fell down. Of course, by then we knew it was an earthquake – all of us had experienced a lot of them – but this was the biggest one we'd felt and it was like, "Oh, oh, that's my house gone." So we all rushed home. But we were lucky that we lived outside the city and my house was fine, just a few missing tiles off the roof. My friends' houses were okay, too. But in the city centre, buildings were down everywhere. My mother took us into San Salvador soon after and it looked like someone had bombed the place. Rubble everywhere, buildings on their side, none of us could believe it. Some of them still haven't been fixed, like that hotel."

Later I found out that San Salvador has an earthquake, on average, every three or four days, most of them in the region of 3 to 4 on the Richter scale. This means they are noticeable, with a little bit of shake, rattle and roll. An earthquake of this strength might be powerful enough to knock stray ornaments off shelves. The one that had felled sections of the city in 1986 measured almost 6, which should not have caused as much damage as it had, but there was one key factor of mid-eighties San Salvador that had made it so devastating: a high proportion of the buildings were of poor quality, especially in the shanty areas.

Little did I know it then, but the next day I would 'experience' an earthquake myself. In the early hours, a tremor measuring 4.6 would strike a region just offshore from El Salvador. I wouldn't notice a thing and neither would anybody else, apart from the scientists who studied such things.

8

We found a parking space near the Metropolitan Cathedral of San Salvador, a huge white-and-yellow edifice that towered high above a busy square. It was one of the biggest buildings in the city. Edgar told me it been rebuilt after the earthquake. Inside was a large picture of a priest, Oscar Romero, a handsome, dark-haired man with a friendly face. In the late 1970s, he was the Archbishop of San Salvador, and had made it his mission to help the poor of the city. By doing so, he greatly annoyed the government, who thought he was meddling In March 1980, while giving a sermon in a hospital chapel, a gunman burst in and shot him dead. He was 62.

The square outside was home to park benches, parked taxis and the obligatory statue of a man on a horse. By my reckoning, it was the busiest place in the city centre, with people everywhere, most of them just passing the time of day by chatting or lounging around. But one other group of people stood out more: the policemen. As Edgar had suggested earlier, they were everywhere, standing on every street corner and intersection, spread out across the centre of the San Salvador every hundred metres or so. In every direction I cared to turn, I could see two, three or four policemen, all watching the people around them. Wearing sky-blue shirts underneath heavily-armoured padding, they looked hard as nails.

"See what I mean?" Edgar laughed, noticing me staring at one particularly mean-looking cop. He was looking right at me, fingertips resting in his pockets near his handcuffs and firearm. But I was glad of his presence; I felt as safe as I could be. With so many law enforcement officers around, there was little chance of a gang member targeting me or my camera.

Just along from us was the National Palace, a grand building bedecked in white columns and fancy window arches. It reminded me a little of Buckingham Palace but, instead of housing the Queen, it contained all the important government ministries. A couple of electricians were laying power cables on the roof. Downtown San Salvador was never going to win awards for beauty, but everything seemed to work in a haphazardly chaotic way. Edgar and I waved goodbye to the square, stepping around the building work in search of sights anew.

9

The melodious sound of Spanish guitars jangled from somewhere up ahead. Edgar and I were crossing a street bursting with ramshackle stores offering key cutting, shoe shining, bag repairs and general kitchen products. Every shop was busy with patrons as if it were a closing-down sale. The guitars grew louder as we took a short cut through an arched walkway. The stores here were selling plastic washing baskets and plant pots. On our left was an ugly wall of corrugated metal, taller than I was. I stood on tiptoe to see what was on the other side and was rewarded with the biggest building site so far. San Salvador's main city square was full of cement mixers, fume-belching trucks and a few cranes. Between the machinery were lengths of pipe and men wearing hard hats.

"It is Plaza Libertad, Liberty Square," Edgar told me. "It used to be the best plaza in the city, full of trees and flowers. Hopefully it will look good again soon. And that statue in the middle – the one covered in scaffolding – is the Monument to the Heroes: to the men and women who fought for our independence against the Spanish." It featured a winged angel holding two laurel wreaths.

The musicians were just ahead of us, limbering up for a performance. Perhaps sensing that they had a tourist in their midst, they suddenly started playing a quick-tempo tune complete with deep resonant singing. We stopped to watch them; I was particularly interested in the fine-fingered dexterity of the guitar players. Quick-changing Spanish-flavoured chords were notoriously difficult to play at the best of times, but cramped up in a narrow corridor, pressed up against a shop-front while an almost endless stream of pedestrians, hawkers, shoe shiners and lottery ticket sellers paraded though, seemed almost impossible. And yet it was not: the troupe sounded mighty fine and so I dropped a handful of coins in their hat.

"They used to play in the plaza over there. But now they're forced to perform here. Same with the pupusa sellers."

"Pupusa?" I had never heard of such a thing.

"The national dish of El Salvador. They are thick tortillas filled with pork or cheese or sometime refried beans, which is my favourite. When I was a boy, my mother made them. All day she would cook pupusas, selling them to our neighbours." Edgar laughed. "When my son was born, all I could think about was giving him his first pupusa. So when he was old enough – and his mother said it was okay – I let him try one. You should have seen him scrunch his face. It was so funny; I can still picture him. He hated them back then. Now, though, they are his favourite thing. Whenever we go out, he's always asking for one. His favourite is pork and cheese. Tomorrow you can try one, if you like."

I nodded absentmindedly; the following day was going to be an interesting one. Edgar was picking me up hellishly early in the morning so he could drive us to Honduras. When we got there (if we got there – the border crossing area was commonly known as 'bandit country'), I should get to see another set of Maya ruins at a small town called Copan. It promised to be an exciting day, now with the added bonus of a pupusa.

We walked on, emerging from the arched walkway into yet another nondescript part of the city. I took no real notice of the ugly, grey concrete edifice in front until we stopped outside its entrance. It was a church, albeit one of the most disagreeable ones I had ever seen. Its bell tower was the worst bit, and at first I thought it was a concrete fire escape. The roof was not much better: a curve of unsightly concrete blocks with tiny holes drilled into it. The whole thing looked fit to be demolished. The large metal gate that formed part of its entrance looked like it belonged outside a Bronx convenience store. The El Rosario Church was an eyesore: an ugly concrete mess that should never have been built.

"Welcome to the most beautiful church in Central America," Edgar said without humour. He waited for his statement to sink in, watching for my reaction. I didn't say anything; I just stared at the drippings of cement visible on the underside of the overhanging roof. Was the man blind?

Edgar said, "Follow me inside and you will see."

And, by God, he was right.

The change from exterior to interior was as immediate and astounding, like swapping a lump of mud for a sparkling sapphire. A rainbow kaleidoscope of reds, greens, oranges, blues and, mostly, golds cascaded from the tiny gaps in the concrete roof and sides. The effect was startling, mesmerising. The pews, the altar and the tiled floor, all were bathed in gorgeous hues of light. It was, simply put, the best church I'd ever been inside. To come up with a treasure trove of light contained within a concrete monstrosity was either the work of a madman or a genius. I took picture after picture, from every conceivable angle, but the interior of the El Rosario Church was too beautiful to represent as an image. You simply have to visit it in person.

10

To get to the volcano, we drove through the outskirts of San Salvador. At one junction, Edgar pointed out the home of a wealthy person. Like the majority of dwellings along the street, the house was two storeys high, large and stout; it had masses of gnarled barbed wire coiled around its graffiti-covered concrete perimeter wall. Instead of being a sanctuary, the upmarket home looked like a prison.

"The wall was because of the civil war," Edgar told me. "See that lamppost there?" He pointed at one standing at the intersection. "In the 1980s, guerrillas used to come down from the hills to tie explosives to lampposts. Every time the bombs went off, the surrounding buildings would get damaged, so that's why they all ended up with these concrete walls."

Our road quickly turned into a mountainside snake. Every once in a while, we had to slow behind a chicken bus or a truck packed to high heaven with people. As we passed one truck, I saw perhaps thirty people squeezed into the rear open-air compartment: pensioners were towards the front, younger men at the rear were holding onto the overhead bar with all their might. If they lost their grip, they would tumble out into the road.

There were plenty of school kids walking the route, too, all of them in white shirts and grey shorts or skirts. Some stuck their arms out hoping that the vans or buses would stop for them. None did because they were already bursting full. I checked my watch. It was close to 5 p.m., so the kids were finishing late, but Edgar explained that children in El Salvador went to school in two shifts – morning or afternoon. "There's not meant to be any difference in the shifts, but most parents know that the kids who go in the morning are usually cleverer or more trustworthy. They are more alert in the morning. My son goes in the morning shift. I hope it stays that way."

We pulled over on a hillside ledge where a large restaurant looked out across the view. Next to the restaurant was a lookout point where some hip-hop music blared from small speakers. The owners of the speakers were some teenagers lounging around in their cars. They regarded us for a moment, discounted us as harmless and carried on with their conversations.

Below us, stretching from left to right across the whole horizon was San Salvador: a quilt of white buildings nestled into patchworks of green hills. From up here, it was hard to imagine that somewhere down there lived two of the most dangerous gangs in the world.

"So will there be any killings today, do you think?" I asked.

"Almost certainly. I read somewhere that the city has a murder every hour. There might be one happening right now."

We got back in the car and drove up to the volcano parking area. At one end was a life-sized cardboard mock-up of a chicken bus. After I posed in the driver's seat for the cheesiest photo of my trip so far, Edgar and I began the hike up to the crater. It wasn't that far, but the route took us through thick jungle busy with fluttering butterflies, drooping flowers and impossibly tall trees, so I was still sweating like a baboon by the time we reached the viewing platform. Edgar had fared better, but was still out of breath. "The light is not on our side," he said as we walked to the edge. "It is always better in the morning."

I gazed down into the volcanic crater. If I hadn't known it was a crater, I wouldn't have given it a second glance. To me, it looked like a deep, hazy valley thick with trees. I could hardly see the bottom due to the sun's glare. It was nothing like the lava-frothing fissure for which I'd been hoping.

"It was formed about one thousand years ago," Edgar informed me, switching seamlessly into guide mode. "The volcano blew its top leaving this round crater. It is 1.5 kilometres across and five hundred metres deep. It used to be full of water; people used to swim and row their boats down there. But in 1917, like I mentioned earlier, the volcano woke up and evaporated the lake." Edgar shielded his eyes to peer downwards. He pointed to the middle of the giant caldera where I could just about make a smaller circle, which was actually a small volcanic cone. "The baby one," as Edgar called it, "formed during the 1917 eruption. It's only thirty metres high."

More interesting than the caldera was a large bird of prey flying above the caldera. To me, it looked like an eagle, but Edgar told me it was a turkey vulture.

"How can you tell?" I asked.

"The size is the biggest clue. The wingtips are another. Black vultures have white wingtips. But this one doesn't."

"But how do you know it's not an eagle or a hawk or something?"

"Its head. Vultures have small heads."

I studied the bird soaring effortlessly above the giant hole. Its head did look small, but no smaller than any other bird I'd seen. But I took Edgar at his word, watching the vulture riding the thermals without a single beat of its wings.

11

I asked Edgar how he became a guide. We were in the car on our way back down the volcano. The gradient was steep, but the brakes were handling things admirably. Edgar seemed to be one of those special guides who made a client feel completely at ease. I was wondering whether he'd had any special 'people skills' training.

"I used to work in IT, but it was so boring. It was a telecommunications company and the job was not interesting, just checking wires and diagrams all day. So one day, I was in the centre of the city and a man stopped me. He was from Canada and told me he was lost. He wanted to know where his hotel was. So I told him but then decided to show him; it wasn't far and, along the way, I pointed out a few places of interest to him. He seemed interested. And when we got to his hotel, he was so grateful that he offered me money. I didn't take it, but it made me think. I looked into being a tour guide and here I am, fifteen years later. I make more money doing this than I ever did in IT and I get to go out and see things, meet people and be my own boss. I work freelance for the company you booked this tour with. I can pick and choose the jobs I want to suit me."

I could see the appeal, especially the being his own boss part. "But have you had training on how to deal with people."

"What do you mean?"

"Well, I think you're a great guide – one of the best I've had." I explained about how he had put me at ease and had not rushed me.

Edgar looked like he was about to burst into song. "That is such a nice thing to say, Jason. You're so kind. But there is no training for that type of thing. I just … do it. But maybe you could meet my wife and tell her; she is always saying I rush her."

Edgar told me about another course he had attended. "When I first became a guide, work was slow, and my wife was worried about the lack of money. Then tourists – mainly Americans – started asking about bird watching in El Salvador. I didn't know anything about birds, and neither did any of the other guides, which meant a lot of these tourists flew to Costa Rica instead. So I had an idea. I looked into birdwatching courses and found out there was one in Tegucigalpa, the capital of Honduras, so I had to persuade my wife to let me go. She did, but the price was $150, so I then had to persuade my friends to lend me the money because we didn't have any. They gave me the money. I caught a chicken bus all the way to Honduras, which took ten hours. But the course was amazing; I loved it. I came back qualified to spot birds. So when we got another inquiry about birdwatching, I was the one who did it. An American guy came over for four days and all we did was look for birds from dawn until dusk. It was hard work but I loved it. In the end, I think we crossed off about a hundred and seventy species."

"So that's why you were so good at identifying the turkey vulture?"

Edgar smiled. "Birds of prey are easy."

We slowed down on a bend in the hillside and then stopped. To our left was a large house with a statue of an eagle on the roof. Edgar asked whether I knew what type of eagle it was.

"Turkey eagle?"

"No such thing. It's a bald eagle – the symbol of America. The owner of this house is telling his neighbours, or anyone passing, that they made their money in America. They worked over there until they had enough money to buy this house. Other houses around here might have American flags or little Statues of Liberty in their gardens."

I asked whether the neighbours might be jealous.

Edgar pulled a face. "No! They are happy for them. It's a common dream: go to America, find a good job, save up and build a house back home, a place you can retire and leave to the children. So when people see a house like this, it makes them want to make something of their life."

"Would you want to move to America?"

Edgar paused. "No. I have everything here in El Salvador. Besides, I think the price of working in America is too high. I don't want to sacrifice my happiness."

12

The vehicle in front was a standard red pick-up with one key difference: its rear section was brimming with fruit and vegetables. Juicy red tomatoes, tongue-searing chilli peppers, large onions and bags of bulbous potatoes swung from the roof's metal railings. In boxes sat more produce, and sitting amid it all was an apron-clad man gripping on for dear life.

Edgar said, "These guys are a new enterprise in San Salvador. They drive up and down the streets beeping their horns and then they park somewhere, waiting for people to buy their stuff. I think it's a great idea." I watched the pick-up turn onto a residential street where the driver began beeping in earnest. It was like the healthiest ice-cream van in the world, only without the ice-cream.

Fifteen minutes later, we were driving through an upmarket part of the city, a world of glitzy shopping malls, fancy restaurants and high-end hotels. With darkness only half an hour away, it was almost time for the gangs of San Salvador to strut their stuff, but not in District 3, the area Jose and I were passing through. District 3 was one of the safest parts of the city, due to the number of security cameras, armed guards and electrified fences. I looked outside. If I had been teleported here from England and made to guess where I was, I certainly would not have said anywhere in Central America. With its McDonalds', Wendy's and Pizza Huts, not to mention the glass-fronted bank headquarters and art museums, I could have been anywhere in the western world. But then, that is the stark reality of living in a city where the rich and the poor are separated by an accident of birth, hopefully to never meet.

Outside my hotel, I bid Edgar farewell, promising I would set my alarm clock for the early morning start. Thinking about Honduras made me pause for thought again. The Foreign Office website had cautioned about the high levels of crime. In particular, it warned travellers to be careful of armed robbers when crossing the Honduran border. I asked Edgar about this possible danger.

Edgar smiled. "Put it this way, I have done the Copan trip maybe twenty, thirty times. Nothing has ever happened to me or any of my clients. If I believed there was any danger, I would not go. I cannot imagine my wife bringing up our son by herself. And I know about these warnings. Governments want to tell people about every possible thing that could wrong, but honestly, the worst thing that will happen is we get delayed, maybe because of a truck driver's strike or something. Everything will be fine. I'll see you tomorrow at 4.30 a.m."

And with that, I jumped out of the car, grabbed my luggage from the back and settled down for an evening of relaxation tempered by thoughts of Honduran bandits taking me hostage at a remote jungle border.

SAN SALVADOR

TOP: A policeman watching the citizens of downtown San Salvador; A cheesy smile and I could be a Central American bus driver

Middle: A panoramic view of San Salvador; A photo cannot do justice to the beauty of inside the El Rosario Church

Bottom: A musician playing in San Salvador; El Salvador has the best number plates in Central America

Chapter 5. Copan, Honduras

FCO Advice: Crime and violence is a serious problem in Honduras. Attacks can take place anywhere and at any time of the day.

A cacophony of shrill beeps and unearthly jangles went off at 3.50 a.m. I ignored the racket and kept my eyes closed until it ceased. Ten minutes later, it was back, rousing me from my restless slumber, and this time I forced myself out of bed and switched on the light. After staggering to the bathroom, I regarded myself in the mirror. My eyes, demonic, bloodshot and red, seemed unwilling to join in with my Central American fiesta.

Even after a cup of hotel room coffee, I felt almost ill with fatigue. Whose idea was this – to get up at the crack of dawn for an insane road trip through El Salvador, Guatemala and Honduras? It was the plan of a madman, that's who, and that man was me. Without even bothering to open the curtains (what would be the point with the night's cloak tightly covering San Salvador?), I grabbed my hat, wallet and passport, heading for the elevator.

Unlike me, Edgar looked sprightly and alert, which was a good job because he had a lot of driving to do. "Did you sleep well?" he asked me.

I shrugged, trying to force light onto my retinas. "I did until my alarm went off."

"Yes, but it is good we start early. It is a two hour drive to the Guatemalan border, then another two hours to the Honduran border. Then thirty minutes to Tikal."

"So four and a half hours in total?" I wondered whether I'd be able to lie in the back of the car and go to sleep.

Edgar laughed. "No. It will be at least five hours, maybe six. The borders are unpredictable and so is the traffic. Also, the roads in Guatemala are not good – many potholes. But there is plenty to see on the way. And it will give me a chance to explain a little more about the history of El Salvador and Honduras. Okay, if you're ready, we can go."

It was still dark as we set off through the neon-lit streets of San Salvador, stopping at a petrol station to grab supplies for the journey. At the entrance to the shop stood an armed guard, his automatic rifle pointing downwards but his eyes fixed on us as we walked past. Ten seconds later, we were browsing the aisles looking for snacks to keep us going on the long trip. I opted for a couple of energy bars and a banana. Edgar picked up a large bag of boiled sweets. We both ordered coffees. When they came, I guzzled the lukewarm liquid down in seconds, trying to get the caffeine fix into my system. Then I ordered another.

Back in the car, with my eyelids drooping, Edgar sipped on the remains of his coffee. The guard was still watching us with intent. It made me wonder how often he would actually be needed, but Edgar told me his presence was not there to shoot back at the bad guys but to deter them from robbing the shop in the first place.

"Still," I said, "it must be a dangerous job?"

"Maybe, but not as dangerous as being a bus driver in El Salvador. Driving a bus is the most dangerous job a person can have – even more dangerous than being in the police. The newspapers are full of stories about bus drivers being shot and stabbed. It's a wonder anyone wants to do it."

"Why are they being shot?"

"It's to do with extortion. The gangs will ask the bus company owner to pay them a little bit each day – not much, maybe only a dollar or two – as a 'protection' fee. Most of the owners do, but sometimes, one might refuse and then their drivers get shot. It's not just the bus drivers: it's the man selling his vegetables in the cart, the shopkeeper over in District 6 or the lorry driver taking his bread through a gang-controlled area. All of them will have to pay a little bit to one of the gangs just to get by or do business. I read somewhere that seventy percent of all businesses in El Salvador pay the gangs in some way or another, and nearly one hundred percent of the bus companies do. Recently, there was a newspaper report about some poor guy who owned one bus. He refused to pay the extortion and so the gangs waited for three weeks, telling him he had to pay, and now owed three weeks' worth of fines. The guy still refused to pay, making a stand against them, so they shot his driver and then, when he still didn't pay, they shot him like a dog in the street. Do you know how much he owed? Twenty one measly dollars."

Back on the road, the first embers of light were illuminating the horizon, fooling my weary body into thinking that it was time to be awake. As we headed towards the highway, we passed stalls setting up for the day: women hanging bunches of bananas from hooks, others rearranging coconuts or rustling up fried snacks in vats of oil. I wondered how much these stall holders had to pay the gangs to keep their businesses running. And then we hit the Pan American Highway, a stretch of road that started in Argentina and ran all the way through Central America and into Mexico and the United States. Its name was an evocative one, suggesting endless opportunities and sights as it threaded its way northwards, but the reality was that it was just another road, and one we were not even going to be on for long. Instead, with the morning now almost fully upon us, Edgar and I left the highway, and headed in a north-westerly direction. Ahead of us, somewhere, was the Guatemalan border.

2

An hour away from San Salvador was Santa Ana, El Salvador's second largest city. Edgar suggested we stop for a short while so I could see what it was like. "If all you see is San Salvador, you will not have a full picture of what my country is like."

Santa Ana was in the heart of the coffee growing area; its surrounding countryside was full of emerald rolling hills and terraces, backed by dramatic volcanic peaks. The road leading to it was lined with trees bent over at such an angle that they formed a foliage-laden roof for us to travel under. It was a pleasing way to start our visit.

The outskirts of the city looked like San Salvador – motels, petrol stations and shopping malls, but the centre was gorgeous, an area dominated by three fine buildings: a huge white cathedral, a pastel-green theatre and a large, yellow city hall. We got out and had a wander around all three, passing through a park in the centre which, despite the early hour, was busy with dog walkers and people sitting on benches. From hidden speakers, jaunty accordion music was playing; it sounded like we were in Paris. The cathedral, over a century old, was the best building of the three, adorned with Gothic spikes and spires around its arched windows. It added a touch of class to the whole central core.

"Does Santa Ana have gangs?" I asked.

Edgar nodded. "It's the same as everywhere else. They have turf war battles – each gang wants to hold onto its territory or grab some more – so they can extort all the businesses. So this city has shootings and murders – just like San Salvador – and a few kidnappings, too. It's a shame; before the civil war, Santa Ana was a rich city – maybe the richest in the country; a place where the wealthy coffee businessmen built their grand homes. But during the war, people emigrated, and then the gangs came. They kidnapped the coffee owners, sometimes killed their families. Most decided to leave. But at least the old centre has remained."

Back on the road, we continued towards the Guatemalan border, an hour away, according to Jose. Ahead of us was a truck emblazoned with the word Bimbo. I couldn't help but snigger. Edgar gave me a look. "Bimbo? What's funny? It's just a bread company."

I offered him the alternative meaning from the UK, the one that described a bimbo as a woman who wore tight clothes (especially around the chest area) and lots of make-up, who often had a lower-than-average intelligence. Edgar considered this. "So in your country, bimbo women have big boobs and small brains. Is that what you're saying?"

I nodded.

"And it is acceptable to call these women this?"

I laughed. "No. Not to their faces, at least. It's … an insult."

Edgar looked thoughtful. "So it would not be okay to say: 'Hey bimbo woman! Come here.'"

I laughed at the term 'bimbo woman'. "No, that would be a *bad* thing to say!"

"So the bimbo women don't like it? I think I understand. So are there lots of bimbo women in England?"

"A few."

"What about the United States?"

"Probably some there as well."

"So I am wondering whether I've met any bimbo women myself. Maybe I've had a bimbo woman in this car; I have shown many Americans around."

I couldn't help but snigger. "Look, Edgar, you don't need to say 'women' after the word bimbo. Bimbo is enough to tell a person what it represents." The whole conversation was taking on a surreal quality. And so the journey continued.

3

"A drug cartel is in operation around here," Edgar said. We were still in El Salvador, but closing in on the Guatemalan border, passing through the small town of Texis. "But this cartel is not as violent as the ones further north. Their cocaine-smuggling empire is run like a legitimate business, almost. The police leave them alone."

I looked outside, hoping to see some drug runners in the distance, with bags of cocaine slung over their shoulders but, of course, I couldn't see anyone like that. The town of Texis looked just like another small Salvadoran town: a few houses, a church, some shops and plenty of trees. But Edgar told me that behind the town, in the ranches and haciendas, the gangs were in action. When the drugs arrived from Honduras, the Cartel de Texis sent it overland to Guatemala via a network of unmarked trails.

Ahead of us was a range of mountains that formed the natural borders between El Salvador, Guatemala and Honduras. All three nations came to a point inside a national park and it was possible to climb a hill in the park where all borders met. As we headed up a gradual gradient, flanked with green countryside and hills, I asked Edgar his opinion of his neighbours.

"Good question. Guatemala is our friend. My country had good relations with them. But if we had to choose an enemy, I think most people would pick Honduras. Have you heard of the Football War?"

The term struck a memory somewhere, but I could not recall what it was, so Edgar filled in the gaps.

"Honduras is five times bigger than El Salvador, but has far fewer people. So people from El Salvador naturally migrated across the border where there was more room for them to grow their crops and raise their families. Eventually – and this was back in the 1960s – a fifth of Honduras' population was made up of Salvadorans. But the Hondurans didn't like this, saying that there were not enough jobs for them. So the Honduran government started sending people back to El Salvador. This was the root cause of the Football War: animosity between El Salvador and Honduras because of this forced migration."

Edgar told me that in 1969 things came to a head. Honduras and El Salvador were drawn to play a World Cup qualifying match against each other. "The first game was played in Honduras, and they won. There was a bit of fighting because of this, but not too much. The second game was in El Salvador, and we won. This time there was lots of fighting, but only between the fans. But then the government of Honduras got involved and started sending more Salvadorans back across the border, sometimes by force. Some people were murdered. But anyway, the score was now one game each so they needed to play a decider, which both teams agreed to hold in Mexico City – somewhere neutral. But on the day of the match, my country severed diplomatic ties with Honduras; we wanted an apology from Honduras about the way they were handling the border crisis. No apology came. So on the day of the football match, people from both countries wondered what would happen."

What happened was this: the match went into extra time and then El Salvador won 3-2. Two weeks later, festering relations between both nations soured and El Salvador declared war and invaded Honduras. Thousands of troops stormed the border and, in the fighting, thousands died on both sides. "But it only lasted a few days," Edgar told me. "And then there was a ceasefire. And then things slowly returned to normal. Except for one thing – the Salvadorans who came home didn't have any jobs or money. There were thousands of them, all homeless and they needed help. And this is where my government failed big time. They didn't look after these refugees properly, which eventually caused massive unrest and is one of the reasons that the civil war started a decade later."

"So how are relations between you and Honduras now?"

"Okay, mostly. But both governments are still wary. In 2013, we thought there might be another war because of territory issues but, thank God, it never happened. I can't imagine what would have happened if another war started. Can you imagine tourists wanting to visit El Salvador with a war going on?"

4

The El Salvador-Guatemala border was a jumble of parking bays, confusing immigration hatches and loitering truck drivers. A few chickens were pecking the ground on the opposite side of the road and I watched them, waiting for Edgar to negotiate my exit from El Salvador. When he summoned me, I handed my passport over to a grim official behind one of the hatches, a man who stamped me out with neither a smile nor a sound. That done, we drove through no-man's-land to Guatemala. It was more of the same, with the added bonus of some moneychangers hanging around with rolls of quetzals in their hands. We ignored them, I got my passport stamped again and we went on our way, passing lines of Guatemalan-registered trucks waiting to be allowed into El Salvador.

Within minutes of leaving the border, the road changed from smooth (as it had been everywhere in El Salvador) into pot-hole hell that slowed us down from the start. Edgar tutted as he slowed to less than a walking pace to go over a crack that cut across the entire width of the road. "Like I said yesterday, I've done this trip maybe thirty times over the last five or six years, and the road has never been repaired. It just gets worse; it's like they don't care."

The first Guatemalan town we drove though was Quezaltepeque, whose best feature was its name. After the fine towns of El Salvador, this small settlement of just a few thousand looked ramshackle and neglected, much like the road that cleaved it in two. An hour later, we were at the next border, and the one where I was most likely to come to harm, especially on the side leading into Honduras.

The Guatemala-Honduras border was far busier than the earlier one. About a hundred trucks were parked there, creating one lane of gridlock, all of them waiting for customs officials to check their paperwork, their loads and their driver's credentials. For most of the trucks, this process took days. As well as the heavy goods vehicles, there were old buses and a constant stream of cars. When I climbed out of Edgar's car, keeping a wary eye out for kidnappers, the whole border smelled of diesel fumes and prime incompetence. Officials on both sides of the border seemed to be doing nothing or, if they were, they did it slowly and reluctantly. The result was people waiting for no reason. Many had slumped onto the ground to wait their turn. A white-T-shirted immigration officer on the Honduras side seemed particularly bad-tempered and reticent. Only at the insistence of Edgar did he take my passport and put it in his scanner, and even then without a smile or an acknowledgement of my presence.

In 2014, this particular stretch of road along the Guatemalan-Honduran border was known as the Corridor of Violence, the most dangerous place in Central America. With Mexican drug cartels in control of both sides of the border, the dons were the de facto authority of the land, dishing out their own brand of law and retribution. In 2014, I would not have attempted to cross through, but today, the crime had dropped to manageable levels.

While I waited for Edgar to use the toilet, I found a post to lean against from which to survey my surroundings. Apart from a few loitering truck drivers and a busload of passengers walking towards an immigration office, the long stretch of road didn't look too threatening. Certainly there were no men with guns to shoot me or lengths of pipe with which to cosh me into their getaway vehicles. There were no people surreptitiously glancing at me from behind newspapers and neither were there any unshaven men loading bags of powder in minivans. No, despite the warnings given by the UK Foreign Office, the Guatemala-Honduras border was just a smelly and dusty bottleneck of unorganised chaos.

"So I didn't get kidnapped," I said. We were back in the car, passing a large white sign that read: *Bienvenido a Honduras*, Welcome to Honduras. Truck drivers were chatting next to their vehicles, some drinking from flasks.

Edgar smirked. "Do you think these people have time to plot your kidnap? They are too busy trying to get across this border so they can make a living."

We came to a sudden stop. In front, the road had turned into a truck park. Both verges of the two-lane highway were taken up by trucks waiting to enter Guatemala. A thin section of road in the middle remained for everyone else. But the problem was that some traffic had met head on and everything had come to a standstill.

Edgar seemed to take things in his stride. "This is what I expected. I'm surprised it has taken this long to reach a traffic jam. But we will just wait; eventually things will sort themselves out."

Half an hour later, we still had not moved; the only vehicles that could squeeze past were motorcycles. To pass the time, I watched a pot-bellied truck driver walk up to the next lorry to chat to the driver.

His pal climbed down and they both lit cigarettes. It really was the most interesting action taking place.

"Look, Jason – there's another turkey vulture," said Edgar. I looked away from the fat truckers and saw the bird, high in the sky circling the madness below its wings.

"Do they ever rest? All they seem to do is fly around."

"They rest in trees. You will see plenty of them roosting on the way to Copan. It's strange, you will see a tree – no birds, then the next tree, no birds, then another tree – the same type as all the others – there will be ten, maybe fifteen turkey vultures in it."

"Why?"

"I do not know."

And then, before my eyes could even drop from the sky, the road ahead cleared. We were free to enter the badlands of Honduras.

5

The term banana republic was first coined to describe Honduras. In 1904, a scholarly American gentleman who went by the name of William Sydney Porter wrote a book. In it, he referred to a fictional country as a banana republic, due to the fact that the nation was dependent on the fruity cash crop. Not only that, this fictitious country was at the mercy of US fruit companies who wanted to bleed the nation dry. It wasn't hard to work out Porter's influence; he had just returned from Honduras.

By the turn of the twentieth century, bananas still dominated the Honduran economy, and in charge of their planting, cultivation and export were real American companies, with names such as the Tropical Trading And Transport Company and the United Fruit Company. These corporations effectively controlled all the ports and transports routes in Honduras and, as a result, held enormous amounts of power. They even persuaded the governments of Honduras and Guatemala to sell vast swathes (and we're talking millions of acres here) of land to them, effectively creating their own states within a state. And in these fruit fiefdoms, they took all the profit and gave nothing back to the local communities except misery.

Today, the term 'banana republic' defines any nation overly reliant on one resource: a resource usually held by foreign businesses. Many counties in Africa and Asia are regarded as banana republics (e.g. Zambia for its copper, Botswana for its diamonds and Bangladesh for its jute), but Honduras has managed to shake off the term. Today, less than five percent of its economy is based on banana cultivation; nowadays, coffee and clothing are its biggest sources of revenue. And maybe drugs.

Three things struck me about the portion of rural Honduras upon which we were travelling. Number one: quad bikes. People in Honduras seemed to use them as their family vehicle. Middle-aged women, old men and teenagers were all using them on the road, some with shopping bags nestled between their knees. Quad bikes, it seemed, were the vehicle of choice for Honduran villagers. Number two: men wearing cowboy hats. They were everywhere: riding on horses, waiting for buses, driving buses or quad bikes or simply walking along the dusty road verge; it was as if I was in the Wild West. Number three was the most worrying: it was the number of machetes I could see. Gangs of men brandishing large choppers were marching along the side of the road. Sometimes one would gaze up at the sun, pull his hat down and then take a half-arsed swipe at some foliage. Each machete was perhaps a foot long and looked like it could sever a head with one flash of its grisly blade.

"They are agricultural workers," Edgar said. "They clear the weeds, maybe slice the oranges down from the trees, but mostly they cut corn. These men will turn up at a farm in the morning, hoping the farmer gives them work. This is what they're doing; they are walking to a nearby corn farm."

"Do they ever fight with the machetes?"

"No, except maybe when they are drunk."

I looked outside at a man with a bushy moustache walking by himself. By his side was a large machete, the morning sunlight glinting off its lengthy blade. He didn't look like a murderer; he looked like a man about to chop crops. But when he caught my eye, he did a quick slicing motion across his neck. He then laughed uproariously and traipsed off into a field.

Fifteen minutes later, something was lying by the side of the road ahead of us. At first I thought it was a dead dog, perhaps slaughtered by the Honduran mental patient, but the animal was much larger. It was a dead cow, with a horrendous gaping wound in its side. The wound was too severe for a machete; it looked like a pack of jaguars had been at it, but Edgar told me it had been hit by a truck. "And it must have just happened; there are no vultures."

Thankfully, I didn't have time to dwell upon the gruesome sight as it was already receding into the distance. But then I spotted something else. "Look," I said. "Turkey vultures!" Five or six of the scrawny birds were roosting by the side of the road, and I was excited to have noticed them before Edgar. He'd already pointed out a tree full of them about a mile back but these lazy ones were pecking around in the dirt, their naked, bobbing heads making them distinctly unappealing.

Edgar slowed down and peered through his window. "No, Jason. They are not turkey vultures; they are turkeys." He sniggered.

I studied them carefully. He was right. They were plain old common-or-garden turkeys. My days as a bird spotter were well and truly over. Then we passed a road sign. It told us that the town of Copan Ruinas was close by.

6

From what I saw from the car window, the town of Copan Ruinas looked deliciously pretty. It was full of cobblestone streets, quaint well-kept buildings and men with cowboy hats. Zipping around them were squadrons of red tuk-tuks. At a busy junction, an old woman in a white apron was carrying a large basket of bananas. She waited for a quad bike to pass and then resumed her journey, as did we. In the centre was a Wild West saloon. Outside its entrance stood three men, each wearing an open-necked shirt and a cowboy hat. If the scene had been viewed in black and white, and with a horse or two in the background, it could have been a Californian gold rush town. And I lapped it all up.

"Bimbo!" said Edgar excitedly. He slowed the car to allow the woman to cross in front of us. He was right. The woman was classic bimbo material: big-boobs, high heels and tight clothes. And then Edgar did something shocking. Like a white transit van driver, he lowered his window and looked like he was about to shout something disparaging.

"No," I said. "She's not a bimbo. She's not wearing enough make-up."

Edgar looked at me. "Really? I thought she was a real bimbo woman ... but if you say she is not, then I must be mistaken." The window went back up and we drove past the woman, who was now entering a café.

As her tight behind disappeared through the door I said, "No, I think you were right, Edgar. She was a bimbo."

Edgar nodded. "I thought so. The way you described the bimbo women I thought I was right. I've been looking for a bimbo woman for a while and she was the best one I've seen."

We drove on for a few seconds. "What were you going to say to her?"

"Say to who?"

"The bimbo."

Edgar looked confused. "Why would I say anything to her?"

"So why did you lower your window?"

Edgar looked confused again, then suddenly didn't. "I was letting a mosquito out."

Our primary destination was at the edge of the town, where the car park was almost full. While Edgar went to buy tickets, I surveyed Honduras, a country with the second-highest murder rate in the world after El Salvador. From where I was standing it looked friendly, especially with the gap-toothed cowboy standing across from me. The old geezer possessed a smile almost as wide as his hat. When I smiled back, he shuffled over.

"Hola, amigo, necesitas un collar o una baratija para to esposa?" he babbled.

I didn't understand a word, so gave my stock response. "No hablo espanol, siento." *I don't speak Spanish, sorry.*

The man babbled some more and pointed at a stall. It was covered in a range of touristy things. I shook my head and the man nodded resignedly and waddled away. Edgar returned with another man, a tall, thin gent in a white shirt and a cowboy hat. Instead of spurs and a bullet belt, he had a long stick and a nametag which told me he was Herman: an official guide. We shook hands and the first thing that struck me was Herman's accent. It was so Americanised that I thought he might be from there.

"No," he drawled, "Never been there. I musta watched too much TV, you know. Plus, we get plenty of American tourists coming here. But no one's ever said I sound like I'm from the States before. Anyway, let's go look at the ruins. There's a lot to see."

I arranged to meet Edgar by the exit in a couple of hours.

7

There were more tourists than I expected. A couple of school parties had swelled numbers; most of the teenagers were hanging around the entrance staring into phones. I was the only westerner, but was thankful that no one appeared to be sizing me up for the back of a kidnap van. I followed Herman past a model of the whole site, which showed just how spread out the ruins were. They covered an area of ten square miles. Beyond the model lay a dusty trail that snaked through a forest. There were no signs of the ruins yet.

"So you live in San Salvador?" asked Herman as we took the path.

"No, I'm from the UK. I was just staying in San Salvador last night."

Herman seemed to consider this. "So you came all this way? That musta been an early start?"

"It was. We set off at about 4.30 a.m."

The guide whistled. "Tell me, what did you think of San Salvador?"

"Well, there's a lot of building work going on, and there were police everywhere, but everyone's friendly. Have you been there?"

"No way! I wouldn't go to El Salvador ever. Too dangerous, man! I know we have our problems here in Honduras, but they take it to another level."

I nodded, thinking about something. Time and time again on this trip, the people of one nation had described a neighbouring country as dangerous. Belizeans thought they were better than Guatemalans, Guatemalans believed they were better that Hondurans. And now a person from Honduras was saying that the people over in El Salvador were a bunch of cut-throats. Everyone, it seemed, genuinely believed that their slice of Central America was better than the one across the border, which was, I reckoned, a good thing. If everyone thought the grass was greener over the other side, then no one would stay at home.

Herman continued. "People in Honduras work hard to better themselves. People in El Salvador take it easy. Same with the Guatemalans. They wake up late, take long siestas and then complain when they have no money."

I nodded again. We were still on the trail that led to the ruins and mosquitoes were everywhere. "What about the other countries of Central America? Have you been to any of them?

"No. I want to go to Panama one day, though."

"What about Costa Rica?"

Herman scrunched his face. "I've heard they think they're better than everyone else in Central America because they've got money."

"But Panama has money, doesn't it?"

"Yeah, but Panamanians are different. They don't think like the Costa Ricans. They're happy for one thing. They love to party."

Herman was closed-minded, forming his opinions from what he had heard or read rather than from what he had actually experienced. But there were millions of people just like him, victims of social immobility, unable to see other nations with their own eyes due to a lack of money, time or will. When people such as Herman read a newspaper that talked about gang violence across the border, what else were they supposed to think? So for me, being able to visit all these countries was an amazing deal: I could see with my own eyes just how similar the people who lived in them actually were. At the end of the day, a person from Honduras or Panama wanted the same thing: to be able to provide for their family and to have a bit of downtime on a weekend.

We carried on walking to the end of the trail. Two men who looked ready for slumber checked our tickets and waved us through. And then I sighted my first macaw, its long tail, vivid red plumage and blue and yellow wings making it unmistakable. It was as beautiful as a turkey vulture was ugly.

Scarlet macaws are famous at Copan. They squawk, honk and flap their colourful wings between the tall trees that surround the old Maya buildings. Indeed, to the Maya, scarlet macaws were sacred, representing the sun, and were depicted on many of their carvings. But this one was walking along a fence. Another was perched on the ground eating a corn on the cob. With a chunk of the yellow corn clasped in one of its sharp toes, the macaw was digging in with its impressive beak.

"Are they wild?" I asked Herman, who was patiently waiting for me to take some photos.

"Yes, they are maniacs."

I shot him a glance.

"Joke," he said. "A bad one, clearly. But yes, they are wild in the sense that they can fly wherever they want, but they are tame because they seldom do. They get food here and so they stay.

Sometimes they are a nuisance, though, especially when they fight in the trees. Their screams can carry for many miles. But they sure look good."

Beyond the macaws, we entered a denser area of forest, where the canopy blocked almost all the light. The mosquitoes were thicker, buzzing around ponds and moist rocks and sometimes landing on my bare arms. The rocks and scree slopes that flanked the trail were coated in a veneer of green moss and, beneath our feet, exposed tree roots cut through the path. Ahead of us was a series of stone steps leading to a thick tangle of branches at the top of a hill. Before we climbed them, Herman pointed out one of the rocks littering the side of the path. It looked like all the other moss-covered rocks – except when viewed from the front. It was a skull, complete with two sunken eye sockets. It had been dislodged from one of the unseen temples above us. "Archaeologists are still trying to figure out where it goes."

"So why don't they move it and keep it somewhere safe? Anyone could pick it up and steal it. It would easily fit in someone's backpack."

Herman shrugged. He didn't offer an opinion; instead, he led me to the start of the steps.

8

Archaeologists think the first stone structures in Copan were built in the ninth century BC, the same time period in which a Greek poet called Homer was writing his Odyssey and, somewhere in Central Europe, people were smelting iron ore for the first time. But it wasn't until the following century that this sporadic building work morphed into the great city state of Copan. When it did, the Maya needed a king and the person they picked was K'inich Yak K'uk' Mo', a name which most people thought a bit of a mouthful so they called him the Great Sun Quetzal Macaw I instead.

History tells us that Macaw I was the hippest of all the Maya leaders, at least judging by an incense burner found at Copan that depicted his likeness. In it, K'inich Yak K'uk' Mo' looked like he was wearing the funkiest gimp costume in the shop. He was bare-chested, draped with an adornment of beads and shoulder plates and, on his head, wearing what looked like a gateau with severed hands acting as filling. His mouth looked like it had been sewn shut, and his earlobes had been filled with bolts. Oddest of all were his eyes. Ridiculously large circles, they reminded me of Elton John's look in the early seventies (an image of him is on the front cover of this book so you can see for yourself). Of course, scientists cannot be completely sure that the incense burner is a depiction of K'inich Yak K'uk' Mo', but they are pretty confident; inside his burial tomb, littered around the royal skeleton, they found a goggle-eyed headdress.

A succession of rulers came to power in Copan, among them kings with such names as Jaguar Mirror, Smoke Serpent and the impressively titled Head on Earth. The most famous, though, was Uaxaclajuun Ub'aah K'awill, otherwise known as Eighteen Rabbit. While the Vikings were pillaging the coasts of Northern Europe, Mister Rabbit was building himself a great chamber that allowed for bloodletting sacrifices, a practice the Maya loved. When that was finished, he oversaw the construction of a grand ball court where athletic opponents could battle it out, keeping a heavy ball in the air by using their hips, a game that would end with the winning team being sacrificed, a great honour for any man during Maya times.

During Eighteen Rabbit's reign, twenty thousand people resided within his complex of temples, plazas and royal complexes. Often they would stare up at something called the Hieroglyphic Stairway that detailed all of the important Mayas rulers up to that point. Alas, things didn't end well for Eighteen Rabbit: after he had been on the throne for 43 years, a rival group of Maya captured and beheaded him. The golden age of Copan ended with his death, and, while the Maya population managed to limp on for another hundred years or so, it would never be the same. Eventually, as in Tikal, they gave up and left Copan. By the time the Spanish arrived in the sixteenth century, the site was overgrown and was being used by a few hardy farmers for tethering livestock and growing corn and beans.

Sacrifice was big business in Maya-era Copan. With their love of festivals and feast days, there was nothing the townsfolk enjoyed more than seeing a sacrifice or, failing that, some bloodletting. Barely a day went by without someone being whisked off to a temple for some bloodletting, and when this happened people gathered to watch. The rite usually involved a priest puncturing a soft part of a person's body to obtain a sample of blood. Once collected, the blood would be handed over to the donating person so they could smear it onto whichever idol they were praying to that day. The best kind of blood was from a penis or a vagina, highly prized during Maya times for their association with fertility and growth. So, if a farmer had just planted some corn, he might nip off to the priest, whip his member out and ask for a sharp pin. With his small pool of blood, he would wipe the ground where he had planted his crops. But sometimes the bloodletting was on a grander scale. Occasionally, troops of naked men and women were made to line up side-by-side for mass bloodletting. While a steady-handed priest punctured them in their most private of places, threading everyone together with string, the subjects took solace in the fact that the gods were surely noticing their bloody ministrations.

Even better than bloodletting were sacrifice ceremonies. As well as sacrificing each other, the Maya liked sacrificing animals, and it didn't matter which type. Deer and birds were commonly killed. Less common were the sacrifices of jaguars and alligators, possibly because they were so hard to catch. Animals and people were usually sacrificed in one of three ways: they were taken up the steps of a tall temple and shot with an arrow, which was the quick and easy way; they were decapitated, which was also quick but messier, but the favoured method was when the sacrificial victim was laid down on an altar so that a knife-wielding priest could cut out his or her heart.

If the heart was still beating when he pulled it out, the priest had done his job well. With an appreciative crowd, the priest would then fling the corpse down the steps where it was skinned in preparation for the evening festivities. Later that night, while the citizens of Copan were having a merry old time, the priest would wear the thin veneer of human flesh and dance about the plaza pretending a rebirth had occurred. It was always a great way to end the show.

With thoughts of high priests, sharp knives and kings with huge goggle eyes, I followed Herman up the steps that led to the start of the Copan ruins.

9

I gazed at the collection of Maya structures that formed the perimeter of a grassy plaza we were standing in. Most were in a state of disrepair. As in the forest, large stones littered the ground, clearly toppled from above. Tree roots snaked around the trails and pathways. Herman seemed to sense my disappointment. "Though the stones are grey and a bit dirty now, back in the day, they would have been painted in golds and greens, but mainly reds." His eyes turned wistful. "If I had a time machine, I would come back and stand here, invisible. I would watch the jaguars being sacrificed, the men playing their ball games and look at the king sitting up on the high platforms."

Herman pointed upwards. "See that sculpture? Can you tell what it is?"

Inwardly I sighed. It was a guessing game. Playing along, I looked up, studying the carving of a squat man who seemed to be kneeling down. He was holding something which may have been a flaming torch. "Is it a man holding a flaming torch?"

"No. Guess again."

Bother and drat, to use Dick Dastardly's favourite phrase. I studied the carving again. It still looked like a man holding a flaming torch. Or maybe it was a hammer. I guessed at this.

"No, it's a monkey god. The Maya worshipped howler monkeys. As well as this, the monkey god was important to sculptors; they worshipped him above the other gods, hence the statue. And it's not a torch, it's a mace. But, Jason, if you look closely, I think the face looks like someone famous."

I peered at the monkey's face. It looked human-like, with furrowed eyes and a smiling (or grimacing) mouth, but it did not look like anyone I could place. Herman waited, but when it was clear I didn't have a clue, he said the name. And it was amazing: I could indeed see the resemblance, especially when viewed from the side. Somehow, a Maya sculptor had fashioned a likeness of Arnold Schwarzenegger. It was uncanny.

For the next hour, Herman took me on a tour of the whole Copan site where his annoying guessing game continued. When we came to a stone staircase he said, "What do you think that is?" He pointed at a carving at the top of the steps that could have been a hundred things.

"A tongue?" I guessed.

"No. Guess again."

"A snail?" It looked like a snail to me.

"No."

"A caterpillar? Or maybe a shoe?" I was saying random things now.

Herman looked at me like I was a simpleton. "It's a serpent's fang, Jason. Can you not see how it curves down to make the snake's jaws?" I could see no such thing, but nodded like I could and was glad when we moved on. We stopped at a tall, pyramidal temple almost obscured by thick trees and foliage. The central steps of the temple looked in good condition, but the sides were coated in a thick carpet of green moss and lichen. If the steps had not been there, I might have thought the temple was a hill.

"The sides show how the temple was originally found," Herman told me. "When Copan was excavated in the nineteenth century, all the temples were covered in green moss like this, and many of the stones and sculptures were broken on the ground. Bit by bit, they have fixed it up, but there is still much work to be done. As you can see here, only the central steps have been fully restored. But we also have the problem of looting, river erosion, storms and earthquakes here at Copan. Some scientists believe that a terrible earthquake is the main reason why the Maya deserted Copan."

"But people still loot?"

"I'm afraid so. People steal things from new finds. In 1998, thieves broke through some locked barriers and stole a number of things from a newly-discovered tomb. And this …" We stopped by a stone statue of what was probably once a grand-looking jaguar. "Someone stole the head in the 1930s. We think it might be in New York."

"For a museum?"

"No, for someone's private collection."

We wandered into another large plaza where a couple of stone altars sat ominously at each end. Herman told me that jaguars had been sacrificed on them.

"But I thought the sacrifices always happened at the top of the temple steps?"

Herman smiled. "I think it might have been too dangerous to carry a live jaguar up some steps, don't you think? So they did it here, where the king could watch. He sat up there."

"So if I was here with your time machine, what would I see on a normal day?"

Herman looked around, as if imagining the scene. "Women would be weaving or maybe checking the bee hives; the Maya were skilled at producing honey. In the market plazas nearby, people would be trading fruit and vegetables: items such as maize, chilli peppers, onions and avocados. Craftsmen might be chipping away at new sculptures – they didn't have metal tools, so they used sharpened stone. If it was a festival day, people would be gathering to have feasts or to watch the ball games. Afterwards, there would be much dancing and singing. Finally, as the sun went down, they would watch the sacrifices." Herman suddenly stopped speaking and strode off towards some people. Despite the signs telling them not to do so, the foursome was climbing up on the sides of one temple, taking silly photos of each other. As I watched, two young children climbed to the fourth tier of steps and posed for their parents who were now at the base. Dad was cajoling the pair into moving closer together while Mum looked on worriedly.

"Excuse me," said Herman to the adults. "Did you not read the sign?" He pointed to it.

Dad lowered his camera and looked at the sign. Herman repeated the message in Spanish. Both adults turned around and carried on with their photography, totally ignoring the guide. Herman tutted and returned to me. "Sometimes I wish we could still do sacrifices today. I have a long list of people on the list."

In the largest open area so far, known appropriately enough as the Great Plaza, was a series of individually-placed stone monuments known as Stelae. Each one was about twelve feet tall, intricately carved from a single piece of stone, and represented one of the rulers of Copan. Each stone had an exciting name like Stela 12, Stela 17 or Stela J and there were about eighty of them scattered across the Copan ruins, with about a dozen or so in the Great Plaza. Most had scaffolding around them as protection against the elements.

I walked up to Stela H, which was a representation of Eighteen Rabbit. Unlike the first ruler of Copan, Mr Rabbit looked normal, apart from his huge ears. He had other faces carved into his headdress, though, including a scary-looking monkey, a few snakes but no rabbits. But there was a living creature in his cracks: a small scorpion with an impressive stinger. It scuttled out from its hiding place and disappeared around the rear of the stone. When I tried to see where it had gone, I saw another set of creatures instead. Fifteen brown woodlice had arranged themselves into a most curious group, somehow forming an inverted isosceles triangle. They looked like they were protecting each other from attack, perhaps from a scorpion. I pointed out the triangle to Herman, who peered at it.

"They are not woodlice, they are scorpion eggs."

I backed away. There's something quite repulsive about the eggs of a critter and my inquisitiveness evaporated in an instant. Instead, I returned to the front to study the face of Eighteen Rabbit. He looked handsome in a stony sort of way. His expression suggested he had been a wise king; perhaps he was a wistful one, too. Eighteen Rabbit's gaze was fixed upon the near distance, seemingly pondering the group of tourists coming his way. But, as they approached, they seemed more interested in me than in the stone slab. As the group huddled together a few feet away, their guide asked whether I would pose with them.

The sightseers looked local, ranging in age from about six to sixty. They were Guatemalans, the guide told me. "And they would be very happy if you will stand in the middle." The group smiled broadly, already parting so I could join them. The guide arranged us in front of Eighteen Rabbit and, when we were all ready, he took a photo.

It was time to leave Copan. I thanked Herman, giving him a tip for his time. And then, as we walked to the exit, a small furry animal emerged from the undergrowth. At first I thought it was a large squirrel, or perhaps an unusually cute rat, but Herman identified it as an agouti, a rodent similar to a large guinea pig. The creature had found something in the grass and was sitting on its hind legs chomping away. I watched it awhile, also taking note of the pair of scarlet macaws dancing and fluttering towards the trees at the edge of the plaza. It was a good way to end my tour of the ruins.

10

Edgar parked the car on a cobblestoned hill next to a restaurant. Parked just along from us was another Bimbo van, its red lettering there for all to see. After a private little chuckle, we climbed into a hot and steaming Honduras. The centre of Copan town was full of pretty white adobe buildings with red roofs, most of them set upon steep flagged paths such as the one we were on. Behind everything was a backdrop of lush hills and angry volcanoes. Men in cowboy hats were everywhere. If a town could be put forward to epitomise Central America, then my vote would go to Copan Ruinas.

Edgar wanted me to try some pupusa, the El Salvadoran delight he and his family loved to eat on as many occasions as feasibly possible. "The pupusas in this restaurant are not as good as my mother's, but they are close enough. I recommend the refried bean and cheese pupusa, with a few chilli peppers for some heat. But you can get one filled with whatever you like."

The interior of the restaurant was full of potted plants and empty tables. Edgar explained that it was early for most people to eat, which was good for us as we would get quick service. With the menu all in Spanish, I left it to Edgar to order, asking for the pupusa he had recommended, plus a Honduran beer for good measure.

My bottle of beer came first and I appraised its sticker, nodding in appreciation: a pair of Honduran flags on a blue background looked good, with the name Salva Vida (translated as Lifesaver) splashed across them in bold white. Although it was not saving me from anything, it tasted mighty fine.

"Cheers," I said to Edgar, raising my bottle.

"Salud!" he replied, clinking his glass of water. We both took hearty swigs. And then the meal came: two massive plates with folded masses of corn tortilla spilling over the edge of each one. Prising mine apart, I spied the telltale purple-brown colour of the refried beans, together with the creamy white of some cheese in the middle. A side bowl of hot-looking chilli peppers was already being scavenged by Edgar. As for me, I ignored the chillies and cut off a chunk of pupusa. With Edgar watching me, I popped it in my mouth and chewed on the thick tortilla, finding it heavy and creamy. It wasn't bad but it wasn't something I thought amazing. It tasted how it looked: functional and basic. Even so, I could hardly say that to Edgar, especially since he'd gone out of his way to find me a place in Honduras that served pupusa, and so I lied and told him it was delicious. To prove this point, I cut off another section and added a tiny morsel of chilli on top for good measure. Edgar was tucking in by this point, with the gusto of a man eating his favourite food. In the end, I managed to eat two thirds before claiming I was too full for more. Edgar nodded, stuffing his face until every last molecule on his plate had been devoured.

"How much are they?" I asked. The least I could do was pay for the meal, I felt.

Edgar picked up the menu. "Thirty-five lempira each, plus drinks."

Thirty-five lempira was just over a pound: a bargain.

After lunch, Edgar led me around a busy indoor market. Men were shopping with their wives, who held court with the fruit and vegetable vendors. The market was small but busy, with potatoes, bananas, peppers, cucumbers, tomatoes and cassava trading hands every few seconds. The smell was delicious. Outside was the town's central square, another area of gorgeousness. It was surrounded by a museum, a small church, the city hall, a colonial hotel and a few restaurants. A trio of young men (not in cowboy hats, I noted) were sitting on a bench. Each wore long, pointed shoes made from what looked like snakeskin. To me, the shoes looked ridiculous, like something from the 1950s. When we passed, the men smiled and I smiled back. And then I mentally shook my head. To think that people didn't visit Honduras because they thought it was dangerous, that they might be kidnapped or murdered: how absurd! The town of Copan Ruinas was a calming place of simple, understated beauty. It might just be my favourite town in Central America.

11

"I think it wise we stop at a supermarket before we head back to San Salvador," Edgar suggested. "We can buy some provisions. As you know, it will be close to five hours before we get back to your hotel."

Copan Ruinas only had one supermarket and its car park was full to bursting. Clearly the people of the town preferred afternoon shopping, because the man in charge of the car park was having a hard time controlling the flow.

The Despensa Familiar Store was small but busy. The aisles were full of corn products, eggs and packets of chilli peppers. I bought a couple of Snickers bars and a bag of crisps; Edgar went for a bread roll and some cheese. At the counter, I paid for everything, handing over a hundred lempira banknote. My change came, but I mishandled it and coins spilled everywhere, rolling and clattering on the floor. And thus began the Great Supermarket Coin Chase.

Virtually every customer in the vicinity scrambled to locate the missing change, not to claim the coins as their own but to find them for me. One cowboy was on his hands and knees, stretching underneath a display of toothpaste. He came out with a 20 centavos coin, worth less than half a pence. Another man found a 10 centavos coin. A woman located another coin. Soon all the coins were passed to me and I thanked everybody profusely.

"And people think they are going to be robbed in Honduras," I said to Edgar as we made our way back to the car. "If they could see what just happened."

"I'm sure you don't need me to say this, but most people in the world are kind and thoughtful. The people here in this town are no different to those up in San Pedro or across the border in San Salvador: just normal people trying to make a living. The only problem is that sometimes they have gangs to deal with. And incompetent governments."

And with that, we began our journey back through Guatemala and El Salvador. When we arrived at the hotel five hours later, it was already dark.

"Well, enjoy Nicaragua," Edgar said. "I've heard it's a nice place to visit. Not as good as El Salvador, of course."

I smiled. "To be better than El Salvador, Managua will have to be something special. But I'll tell you something, Edgar; whenever I have high hopes for a country, it sometimes turns out to be the biggest disappointment. I've heard so many good things about Nicaragua that I hope it can live up to the hype. But with El Salvador – and I hope you don't mind me saying this – I had low expectations. Everyone told me I was mad going to El Salvador, that I'd be robbed or murdered. But El Salvador turned out great: better than great, actually, In fact, it's my favourite country of the trip so far. Honduras is a close second."

Edgar considered this. "I'm pleased you enjoyed my country so much. And maybe the word will spread about how much there is to see. You only saw a tiny snapshot. There are many volcanoes and lakes, national parks and beautiful little towns where you could spend hours just wandering. Then there is the Pacific coast. I've been told that some of the best surfing in the world is in Playa Las Flores, a beach to the south of here. We also have Maya ruins, maybe not as impressive as the ones at Copan or Tikal, but still well preserved. You could spend a month in El Salvador and still not see it all."

I shook his hand and promised him I would spread the word about El Salvador.

COPAN

Top: The Honduras cowboys of Copan; Bimbo gave Edgar and me a lot to think about

Middle: One of the many Maya stela at Copan; The centre of Copan Ruinas town; The cathedral in Santa Ana, El Salvador's second largest city

Bottom: A scarlet macaw at Copan; The thorns on the trunk of a kapok tree; the cobblestones and hills of Copan Ruinas

Chapter 6. Managua, Nicaragua

FCO Travel Advice: Street crime is common in Managua. Express kidnappings have occurred involving passengers using unauthorised taxis, where cash is demanded for release a short time later. Don't walk alone after dark.

I was at the airport early for my short flight to Managua. Because of this, another flight was departing the gate before mine. Its destination was San Pedro, a quaint sounding name for a Honduran city up near the border of Guatemala. San Pedro was anything but quaint.

Border towns are always a little bit edgy in Central America. Drugs often pass through and therefore criminal activity is rife. But for San Pedro, the second largest city in Honduras, this activity is notched up to maximum. For as long as most people can remember, the town has been the Murder Capital of the World, regarded by many as the most dangerous place on Earth outside of a warzone, especially if you belong to a gang. Only recently has it been knocked off the top spot, losing out to Acapulco and Caracas.

Drugs gangs are to blame for the horrific homicide rate in San Pedro; on average, it has double the murders of San Salvador (which comes in at number 7 on the hit parade). High unemployment and a lacklustre police force don't help. According to recent statistics, three quarters of all cocaine heading to the United States passes through the Honduran-Guatemalan border, with much of the traffic concentrated through San Pedro.

I looked at the people boarding the San Pedro flight. They all looked perfectly normal: families with young kids, old folk, young couples, businessmen. I couldn't see any tattoos or anyone who looked like a smuggler. But that was the problem, wasn't it? Drug runners and cocaine lynchpins blended in, especially at airports.

I watched a couple of men loading boxes into the San Pedro flight's cargo compartment. When I looked closer, I saw that each box contained oranges. Or did they? Maybe beneath the fruit lay packages of powder. Or maybe my imagination was running away with me. By the time the men had finished loading the fruit, I wondered whether anyone's luggage would fit aboard. But it appeared it could, because lines of luggage were disappearing into the belly. A quarter of an hour later, the flight took off, dead on time.

And then, forty-five minutes after that, the call to board my Avianca flight sounded. After take-off, I calmed down now that I was on my way. Half an hour later, as we descended towards the Nicaraguan capital, I looked outside, taking in the shantytowns. Like many Central American cities, Managua still had plenty of poverty on its periphery. Around a fifth of the city's population subsisted in these barrios, living shoulder-to-shoulder in shacks that crisscrossed water ditches or stood at the edge of dirty lakes. And then they were gone, replaced by another modern Central American city.

After I landed and received my passport stamp, a balding, well-tanned man in his mid-thirties, wearing a white T-shirt and beige trousers, met me outside. His name was Marcus and he was going to be my tour guide for the day.

"Welcome to Nicaragua," Marcus said jovially. "I think we may be in for a bit of rain later on, but hopefully we'll see all the highlights of Managua."

Above the terminal building, the sky was an ominous grey, in direct contrast to the bright sunshine of El Salvador. I smiled. "That sounds great, but what about Granada?" I had booked a trip to see the old colonial capital before seeing Managua. And I thought there was a visit to a volcano, too.

"Granada? I don't know anything about Granada." He shook his head. "Maybe you can check for me."

I took my phone out and scrolled though my emails, quickly finding the information I wanted. It clearly stated that my tour began with an airport pick up, then a trip to Granada, followed by a visit to a volcano before driving back to Managua to see the sights. I showed all this to Marcus.

He read it and shook his head again. "I don't know anything about this. All I was told was to pick you up from the airport and drive you to your hotel, stopping in the city to see a few things. Getting to Granada will take about an hour, plus another hour back. I'm ringing my boss." He sighed and fished in his pocket for his phone. A few minutes later, after a private conversation in Spanish, Marcus nodded. He put his phone away and told me that I was correct. "So let's go to Granada, then." Without waiting for me to say anything, he grabbed my luggage and traipsed off towards his car.

Interesting, I thought as I followed after him: a surly tour guide for the next five or so hours.

2

The Nicaraguan city of Granada holds the distinction of being the first settlement on mainland America taken by the Spanish. During their colonial conquest of the New World, a bushy-bearded explorer called Francisco Cordoba hacked his way through tropical bushes until he found a great lake. Liking what he saw, he planted his flag near the water and named it Granada, after the more famous city in Spain. With this mark of approval, the settlement grew into a town, and then a city, and soon developed into one of the most important trading towns in the region, despite not being on the coast. Instead, it was connected to the Caribbean Sea by the San Juan River, a stretch of water wide enough for trading ships to navigate their way along. Today, Granada is one of the top tourist draws of Nicaragua; as for Francisco Cordoba, the Nicaraguan currency is named after him.

Due to its rich Spanish history – plus the fact that it has largely escaped major earthquake damage – the town is bursting with colonial buildings, tempting restaurants and cobblestone streets. I was looking forward to seeing it, so I could compare Granada to the likes of Flores, Santa Ana and Copan.

"Is Nicaragua a good place to live?" I asked as we drove along. The sky was even darker now, casting dim shadows across the highway. Outside, the scenery was nondescript; beyond the road were fields and hills. The only real diversions were the brightly-painted chicken buses plying the route.

Marcus nodded. "Si, I like it."

I waited for him to add anything, but when nothing more came, I asked him whether he had ever visited any of Nicaragua's neighbouring countries.

"No. I would not ever go to Guatemala or Honduras – too dangerous. El Salvador, too. I've been to Costa Rica and Panama, but they are rich, like us. The others, no way, too many gangs."

"So there are no gangs here in Nicaragua."

"Look, Jason. We have drug problems, but we don't have the gangs that Honduras and El Salvador do. Nicaragua is safe. End of story." We drove on for a minute or so. "You mind if I put the radio on?"

I shrugged. "Go ahead."

And so the journey continued with eighties pop tunes playing, punctuated by the occasional tuneless sing-along from Marcus. Perhaps having to drive me to Granada was seriously pissing him off. And just when I thought things couldn't get any worse, they did. It started to rain.

Heavy drops splattered the windscreen, and soon there were more. Within a minute we were driving through a tropical downpour that reduced outside visibility to grey soup. With the wipers swishing on full blast, Marcus looked almost gratified. "I told you it was going to rain."

I didn't reply, wondering how I was going to make the best of the day with rain and a sour tour guide accompanying my every move. And then, without preamble, we pulled into a Super 7 gas station. "We need fuel," Marcus said, rather needlessly.

While Marcus stepped out under cover of the roof, I regarded the petrol station shop. It was fifteen metres away, but the route was open to the elements. Even so, I decided to risk it, and ran for the door, finding myself soaked to the skin as I stepped into the shop. And then I found it didn't have anything useful to buy, unless I was after engine oil or new windscreen wipers. I ran back to the car, getting another thorough soaking. As I closed the door, I regarded my T-shirt: it was drenched. And so was everything else. So, to add to my woes, I was now wet and cold.

Marcus had another annoying habit I discovered when we set off again. He was one of those men who like to crack their knuckles. He did this frequently as we hit the outskirts of Granada. When small houses began appearing, together with stands selling fruit and vegetables, crack, crack, crack went his knuckles. Most of the stalls were covered in clear plastic as protection against the elements. Horses were everywhere, almost all of them tethered by the side of the road on patches of grass. Most of them had head coverings so they couldn't see how drenched they were getting.

Marcus slowed down and cracked his knuckles again. "Look to your right. See that store?"

I was momentarily stunned, as it was the first thing he had said in a long while. I looked and then nodded. It was a long shop with a selection of its wares hanging outside. I saw what looked like macaws, frogs and sunflowers. Each article was highly colourful and had waterfalls of rainwater dripping from them.

"Can you see what they're made from?"

I studied a large red and yellow macaw. "Wood? Plastic?"

"No, old tyres. The owner collects old tyres that nobody wants, moulds them into animal shapes and then paints them. It's a great idea, I think."

"I agree. He deserves to make a lot of money."

We drove on, with Marcus seemingly in a better mood. Maybe the knuckle-cracking was loosening him up, but whatever it was, he decided to slow down every now and again so he could point out some of the highlights of Granada. We stopped at a couple of churches, a government building and the old Spanish prison. I didn't get out at any of them because, if I had, I would have got saturated. Even lowering the window to take photos resulted in a nasty soaking. And, in contrast to Marcus's sudden jovial mood, mine darkened like the clouds that obstinately hung above Granada. Instead of a bright colonial town, I was seeing a dreary, listless town, with streams flowing over every cobble.

Marcus decided to drive to Lake Nicaragua, the same body of water that Francisco Cordoba had planted his flag next to almost five hundred years previously. It is the largest lake in Central America, with an area of over 8,000 square kilometres, making it about the same size as Cyprus, or 550 times the area of Lake Windermere, England's largest lake. For the ten minutes it took to drive there, the rain got heavier and by the time we arrived the lake was barely visible. All I could see were a few empty pleasure boats tethered by the shore, and one man in the water who looked like he was fishing. Or drowning.

"This is so sad for you, Jason," said Marcus, taking a drag of a cigarette. We were huddled under some thick branches of a tree. "Yesterday, the weather was great. I was showing a Canadian couple around. But that is the luck of the draw. It is the rainy season after all. What can you do?" He glanced at his watch. "It's almost noon, and the rain won't last all day. I think it will be okay for Managua, but the volcano might be disappointing. In bad weather you won't be able to see very much."

"Are there any fish in the lake?" I was watching the fisherman drag a net through the shallow water. He hadn't caught anything, as far as I could tell.

"Oh man, yeah, there are plenty of fish in there. We got swordfish, trout, tilapia. We also get sharks—"

"Sharks?"

"Yeah. Bull sharks. They sometimes attack people."

"But how can they live in a lake? Isn't it fresh water?"

"Yeah, it's fresh water. But bull sharks can live in fresh or salt water. And they get into the lake from the river. Somehow – and don't ask me how – they swim in from the Caribbean Sea along the river until they get to the lake. In the 1960s, the Japanese built a factory by the lake and caught thousands of sharks every year to make shark fin soup. Since then, the number of attacks dropped and so did the sharks. The Japanese packed up and left years ago."

He was right about the sharks; I checked. After a week or two swimming the 120-mile journey along the river, some bull sharks hang about in the lake, snapping up fish or any other type of animal they come across, including people. That said, in the history of shark attacks, only three have occurred in Lake Nicaragua, making it unlikely that the fisherman I was watching would get dragged to a bloody and horrible death.

And so, with the worrying notion of sharks living in lakes reverberating around my mind, we headed back to the car. It was time to head into the town centre.

4

As if the gods knew about my weather-induced despondency, the rain began to ease. At first the deluge morphed into a shower, and then into drizzle. Overhead, the grey layer thinned to white and then revealed some spots of blue. Through these gaps, the sun gushed, splashing warmth and colour onto the streets of Granada.

Preferring to see the sights of the city by myself, I asked Marcus if this would be okay. Marcus seemed more than happy with this arrangement and so, after agreeing to meet by his car in ninety minutes, I wandered off in search of sites, while he went for a cup of coffee and a cigarette at his company's Granada office. The first place of note I found was a large square edged by a park on one side and some grand buildings on the other. Parque Central had all the ingredients of a good square: fountains, palm trees, a bandstand and a nice selection of statues. There was also an obelisk dedicated to the memory of Ruben Dario, a famed Nicaraguan poet who, in his relatively short life, managed to travel the world, have dalliances with scores of beautiful women and then, in his later years, turned to alcohol, which eventually killed him just shy of his fiftieth birthday.

Standing at the far end of the park were some men with horses and carriages. Now the sun was coming out, they were wiping down seats and chrome railings in preparation for sun-seeking customers. Behind them stood the fancy yellow-and-orange façade of the Hotel Alhambra, the oldest such establishment in Granada. Looking at its colonial exterior and promise of a swimming pool, I almost wished I was staying there, but instead I left the park to see the church on the other side.

The Our Lady of the Assumption Cathedral is visible all over the city. Its yellow-and-white triple domes were good, but the rest of it was rather standard in design. But what it lacked in finesse, it made up for in sheer size. It was the biggest place of worship I had seen on my trip so far, and one with a lot of history.

For almost half a century the cathedral (in one form or another) has stood on the south-eastern corner of Parque Central, facing hurricanes, earthquakes and a couple of nasty fires which burned it to the ground. One of the worst fires was started by a notorious, thin-faced, grey-eyed gentleman from Nashville, Tennessee called William Walker. Instead of writing mournful country and western tunes, Walker preferred funding military campaigns, a practice known as filibustering. During the mid-1800s, Walker's grand intention was to conquer vast swathes of Central America in order to take the locals as slaves and make them work the land for free. With a plan sketched out in his head, Walker, plus a couple of dozen paid mercenaries (who all wanted a slice of the slave action) took arms and marched south into Mexico. Astonishingly, this ragtag group of misfits managed to take a small Mexican border town, which Walker promptly declared as the new capital of the Republic of Lower California, a nation he had made up on the spot. After hoisting his new flag, Walker sat back, revelling in his quick victory.

The Mexican government found out what had happened and sent in the army, swiftly kicking Walker and his men out, telling them to never return. Thirty-year-old Walker retreated to the real California, where the American authorities put him on trial for starting an illegal war. But the trial was a sham; the jury was composed of a bunch of slave-owning rednecks who thought Walker a hero. They found him innocent after just eight minutes. And so, after a prudent period of lying low, William Walker decided to invade Nicaragua.

This time, with even more mercenaries wanting to kick some slave ass, Walker timed his invasion with the outbreak of a civil war. In the confusion caused by this, he sided with the team battling the government, even becoming their leader. With his forces significantly bolstered, William Walker took the city of Granada, then the powerhouse of the country. Even Walker was astonished by how well things were going. With this important city in his hands, he set his sights further afield and was soon in charge of huge parts of the country. With victory almost in his grasp, the government of Nicaragua fled, which effectively ended the civil war. Overnight, William Walker found himself in charge of a whole country and declared himself President of Nicaragua. Even the US president at the time endorsed his actions, pleased that an American was leading the way in the wilds of Central America. Walker gave his inaugural speech where Granada's Parque Central's bandstand now sits.

With William Walker's presidency endorsed, he made good his promises and introduced slavery; he also made English the official language. And while this was happening, the neighbouring countries looked on with concern. What if Walker decided to invade them, they pondered nervously? What if he took their citizens as slaves to fuel his personal fiefdom? No, they could not risk that happening. And so Costa Rica, Honduras and El Salvador decided to take Walker on. What choice did they have? The man was clearly off his rocker, so they assembled four thousand troops around the Nicaraguan border, waiting for the order to go in.

The order came, timed to perfection with a sudden outbreak of cholera among Walker's troops. This rendered them almost useless against the advancing army; many defected to the other side, anyway. With foreign soldiers marching towards Granada, hell-bent on crushing his tinpot regime, William Walker strengthened the defences of Granada and then set in motion a dastardly plan.

Walker ordered that the city be set alight. With his cronies setting fires everywhere, soon flames were licking every part of Granada. But the cathedral proved difficult to burn down, and so Walker ordered his men to place gunpowder in its bell towers. When the powder was set alight, the inferno was enormous, reportedly burning for a week, until the cathedral was nothing but a ruin. Only then did Walker open the city gates, lay down his weapons and offer himself to the mercy of the Costa Ricans, Hondurans and Salvadorans. And, unbelievably, instead of stringing him up from the nearest tree, they packed him off to America, where he was hailed a hero. And then, four years later, he was off again, this time to Honduras, where his luck ran out. When the British found he was poking his nose into their business interests, they arrested him and handed the filibuster over to the Honduras authorities. On a warm day in September 1860, William Walker, aged just 36, was executed by firing squad.

5

I decided to get something to eat and found a small café around the corner from the cathedral. After filling up on delicious tortillas, I wandered Granada's pretty streets, discovering attractive lanes lined with pastel-coloured shops and houses. The street signs were great, too. Each corner had a blue-painted sign perched at the intersection, a street name set inside a decorative border. Along one road was the best doorway in town, a fancy wooden entrance that featured a pair of blue toucans, next to an equally pleasing green-and-yellow entranceway. Granada was more than just a splash of colour, it was a veritable kaleidoscope.

I checked my watch and realised my time was up. I found Marcus lounging outside his tour company's office, smoking another cigarette. His break from tour guiding had put him in an even better mood and, as we walked to the car, he was asking me all sorts of things, such as if I'd seen the cathedral and the colourful buildings and if I'd had something to eat. When I told him I'd tried tortilla with a local beer he seemed even more pleased. "A lot of tourists come here and they only try Western food and drink beers like Heineken. It's good that you're trying the local things; it helps the economy."

Marcus told me that we should now visit the Masaya Volcano. "It's a forty-minute drive, but before that, we will visit a little town called Catarina where you can see the Apoyo Lagoon. It is a lake inside a caldera. Do you know what a caldera is?"

I nodded. "It's a volcanic crater. When a volcano erupts, it might leave a round hole behind. I saw one in El Salvador."

"Ah, yes, that's right; your flight came in from San Salvador. Tell me, what was El Salvador like?"

I told him it was great and full of friendly people.

"That is not what I've heard. I've heard it's dangerous. Did you see any gangs?"

"No."

"What about poverty?"

"I didn't see any. But I was only there for a couple of days."

"I think you're a brave man, my friend, going to El Salvador." Marcus looked up at the sky, assessing the weather. It looked like the clouds were regrouping for another assault. It was time to get going.

More or less as soon as we hit the road, the blue sky turned to grey and the rain began its annoying descent. Marcus mentioned that if it got much worse, the volcano would be a washout. "You won't see a thing. You would be staring at nothing."

At the halfway point of the journey, with no easing of the rain, we stopped briefly in the town of Catarina. As we drove past a few unremarkable buildings, Marcus stopped. "See that building there?" he asked, pointing to a large orange building that called itself Bar El Cuartel. It had a nice arch and some attractive lights but, apart from that, it looked normal, like most of the buildings in the centre of the small town. "Look around the door and across the front. Can you see the bullet holes?"

I could, now that they had been pointed out. There were lots of bullet holes, as if someone had fired a machine gun at the wall. "From the revolution," Marcus stated.

"But I thought that ended decades ago."

Marcus shrugged. "It did, and these bullet holes date from 1979. I think the owner likes them. He thinks they give his restaurant character."

We drove out of the town and parked in a little area surrounded by tourist shops and cafés. The rain was hellish now, but enjoying the deluge were a gaggle of geese paddling through a pathway that had turned into a stream. Most people, along with a trio of stray dogs, were huddled together under shop awnings, occasionally sticking their hands out to assess the weather. Marcus fished around in the glove compartment and found a photo. It showed a large blue lake, roughly circular in shape, bounded by lush Nicaraguan countryside. "This is the view you could've seen."

It looked glorious.

"Let's see what it looks like now."

We climbed out and ran for cover. A woman in charge of a stall selling wooden carvings and Nicaraguan flags looked at me hopefully, but resumed her morose vigil of the rain when she saw I had no intention of buying anything. Ten minutes later, with no sign of the torrent easing, Marcus led me from awning to awning, until we rounded a bend and arrived at a scene of pure grey. It was like we were standing in a cloud, because there was nothing to see, absolutely nothing beyond a few benches. Yet it was windy. The cool air blowing up from the unseen lake was whipping my face and sodden T-shirt. "That is the lake," Marcus told me with a hint of sarcasm. "Enjoy the splendour of it." The scene was nothing like the photo he had just shown me.

Nearby was a stall selling food. The woman's fried snacks were covered in clingfilm held down with small pebbles. She looked despondent. Marcus noticed her dejected look and bought some snacks, returning with a two small bags. He passed one to me. "These are *tostones*, fried plantain."

I thanked him and pulled one out. It was the size of a fishcake, flat and round, yellow-beige in colour. It wasn't oily but seemed brittle and so I took a bite. It tasted like a flavourless cracker and so I ate the rest, more out of politeness than need.

"We can wait here to see if the weather clears up," Marcus said, snapping off a section of his snack. "Or we can head to the volcano. But to be honest, I think that's going to be a waste of time, too."

I didn't want to hang around, so told him we might as well try the volcano. If it was a no-go, I could just head back to my hotel in Managua and sign off on what had been a quite unexceptional day.

6

I didn't see the volcano.

Because of the downpour, the people who ran it took the unprecedented step of closing down the whole complex due to danger of slipping. Well that was that, then, I mused. Nicaragua, three: me, nil. There was only one thing left to do and that was drive to Managua where I could at least see some of the famous sights of the city before being deposited at my hotel.

Twenty minutes later, we hit the outskirts of the Nicaraguan capital, the third-largest city in Central America (after Guatemala City and San Salvador) and began a long drive under billboards adverting banks, pizzas and mobile phones. Palm trees added a touch of exoticness, and every so often we would pass massive posters of the Nicaraguan president and his wife.

Daniel Ortega, the president, had a thick black moustache, thinning hair and a friendly expression, like that of a kindly grandfather. His wife looked equally affable, waving at everyone passing the poster. In his early twenties, Daniel Ortega spent seven years in prison for armed robbery. Upon his release, he moved to

Cuba, where he trained as political guerrilla, a favoured occupation for many young men at the time. Upon his return to his homeland, Ortega fell under the spell of a raven-haired beauty called Rosario Murillo, a highly intelligent woman who also had an interest in politics. With her at his side, Daniel Ortega began a political career that quickly catapulted him into the upper echelons of Nicaraguan government. By the end of the 1970s, he found himself leader of the country, a far cry from his humble beginnings as a bank robber.

Daniel Ortega was president of Nicaragua for much of the 1980s but, during the 1990s, he relinquished control to work behind the scenes, with Rosario Murillo orchestrating some carefully-planned moves. In 2007, Ortega made a comeback and won the new presidential election. He won again in 2011 and 2016, and then took the unprecedented move of making Rosario Murillo, his wife of almost forty years, the Vice President of Nicaragua. This was a masterstroke for two reasons. Firstly, she was highly popular in Nicaragua, a champion for the poor and therefore had the backing of the common people. Secondly, because most Nicaraguans knew she had been pulling the strings behind the Ortega government for years anyway, it seemed only fair that she was offered high office. Besides, if anything should happen to the president, she would be poised to take over the top spot.

A massive metal tree caught my eye. It was on the central reservation, curly and red, easily taller than the real trees near it. It looked like a Christmas decoration that hadn't been pulled down, especially with its proliferation of attached light bulbs. When we passed another, a blue one this time, I asked Marcus about them.

"They are the work of the Vice President. She calls them the Trees of Life – she designed them, and I think there are over one hundred in Managua, maybe one hundred and fifty, all identical, except for the colour. They're still being put up."

I got the impression that Marcus wasn't a fan of them. "Do you like them?"

"They're okay. They look good when they're lit up at night, but they cost a lot of money. I've heard that each one costs something like twenty five thousand dollars. So that's millions of dollars for them all. We could build a hospital for that, or maybe make the schools better. So I don't know whether I'm a fan or not. Probably not, especially when they pull a real tree down to make room for one of these fake ones."

"I bet the electricity bill is not cheap either, not if they're lit all night."

Marcus nodded as we approached a roundabout with another of the metal trees on it. "I think the bill is a million dollars a year to keep them lit. But at least we have the electricity to keep them on. I remember not too long back – maybe ten years ago – when we had blackouts all the time. Every day there was a blackout in Managua – sometimes they lasted for five or six hours. If you were walking the street at night and the lights went off, you banged into things or fell into a hole. Man, it was bad. So at least something's going well."

Another thing going well for Nicaragua was tourism. For about a decade, tourism has been the second biggest money-spinner for the country, after coffee growing. With its uncrowded beaches, active volcanoes, beautiful lakes and colonial history, it was something the government was looking to capitalise on further. And it was working, because here I was, seeing the tourist sights of Managua, the first of which was the Metropolitan Cathedral.

7

It was ugly. That was the simplest adjective to describe the hideous, bulbous mass of concrete that made up Managua Metropolitan Cathedral. If it were a nuclear bunker or a bomb factory, then fine, but as the top cathedral of Managua, it was severely lacking. The array of ugly dome things on the roof didn't help; they were like egg boxes sitting on top of an old grey shoebox. Around the side was a weird cylindrical annex, covered with tiny circular holes. What its purpose was, I had no idea. But it looked like a concrete igloo designed to contain a maniac. The only saving grace was that the rain had finally stopped, meaning I could get out of the car.

Leaving Marcus to have another cigarette, I stepped inside the cathedral, standing behind the mostly empty rows of wooden benches that faced a small white altar. The interior was far better than outside, but still nothing special. At the front of the cathedral sat a few worshippers, listening to a priest speaking in Spanish. I left them to it, regarding three bushy-bearded homeless people sitting on a damp wall outside. All three were slurping away on bottles of beer, talking animatedly. When they noticed me, they waved and I waved back, heading back around the corner near the annex. And it was then that I heard the crack of automatic gunfire.

It was shockingly loud. Instead of diving to the ground for cover, I spun around and saw the gunmen. They were not Nicaraguan revolutionaries but teenagers playing with firecrackers. When they witnessed my reaction, they doubled up with laughter. A deep voice shouted from somewhere and the boys legged it.

When my pulse had recovered sufficiently, I noticed something strange on the horizon. It looked like a tall statue on a hill, perhaps a man wearing a wide-brimmed cowboy hat. Next to him was one of the metal trees. When I asked Marcus, he told me we were heading there next. "They're on Tiscapa Hill, and the silhouette statue is Augusto Sandino, one of our national heroes."

The drive up the hill was quick and easy. When we arrived, I found myself the only visitor, apart from a young couple whose prime interest was canoodling by a fence that overlooked the city. Ignoring them, I gazed up at the huge silhouette-like monument to Augusto Sandino, its stark blackness against the overcast sky bold and effective.

Sandino remains one of the most enduring heroes in all Central America. When the Americans were in Nicaragua between 1909 and 1933, Augusto Sandino and his band of guerrillas were a constant source of annoyance. When he began calling himself Caesar, they claimed he was a bandit. Yet they could never catch him. In the end, America pulled out of Nicaragua and a new, home-grown government came to power with Sandino at the helm. Alas, he didn't live long enough to see the fruits of his labour; he was assassinated by the notorious National Guard a year later.

The metal tree next to him looked impressive, too: this one was in white, offering direct contrast to the black statue alongside. It was the closest I'd been to one of the Trees of Life and I studied it for a while. It really was massive, staggeringly so, as tall as a five-storey building. And. as Marcus had told me, it was covered in thousands of light bulbs. But was it actually any good? I thought for a moment and decided that it was. This tree and the others just like it offered splashes of vivid colour in otherwise lacklustre parts of the city. And they did give Managua a bit of identity, albeit an expensive one.

In the shadow of the tree sat a sorry-looking tank, a rusted vehicle that Mussolini had once donated to Nicaragua. The young couple were staring at it, holding hands. I left them and instead looked at the battered ruins of the old National Guard's security office. A ledge looked down upon broken and dirty concrete walls. Jutting sticks of rusting steel and smashed floors with deadly gaps made up the remains of the office. It was exactly how I imagined a building to look following a severe earthquake, which is precisely what happened to it. Just before Christmas 1972, while most of the city was sleeping, an earthquake measuring 6.2 struck thirty kilometres from Managua. For fifteen hellish seconds, the city shook like it had never shook before, toppling almost every building in the city centre and killing thousands of people in the process. It would take more than three decades before things returned to any semblance of normality in Managua. But the National Guard building had never been rebuilt – and why would it have been? The National Guard were a terror militia propping up a Nicaraguan dictatorship that lasted from the 1930s until the revolution of 1979. Before it was toppled, the headquarters was a place where people often went but seldom left. One of the people who did manage to see the inside of the cells and live to tell the tale was Daniel Ortega, current president of Nicaragua, held for revolutionary activities in the 1970s.

I noticed the canoodling couple had departed in a car, leaving only Marcus (who was having another cigarette) and me. I walked to the railing where the romantics had been earlier, seeing a view that stretched across the northern edge of the city (the buildings almost smothered with lush greenery) until it reached the shore of Lake Managua, one of the most polluted lakes in the world. Despite recent efforts at controlling the amount of untreated sewage flowing daily into the lake, it is still called the world's biggest toilet. From my perch, it looked perfectly nice, albeit indistinct, but I knew that if I saw it up close, I would see litter, debris and chemical scum floating in the putrid-smelling water. If I was unlucky enough to fall in and ended up with water in my mouth, I would almost certainly have diarrhoea or worse. Even so, people still eked out a living by the shores of Lake Managua, catching the stunted fish with missing eyes or misshapen fins to sell at ramshackle street markets. As for me, it was time to head down the hill to see the centre of the Nicaraguan capital.

8

As in other Central American countries, female models on advertising billboards were not the stick-thin young women of Europe, but instead ladies of wider berth. None were overweight, of course – quite the contrary – but most of the women would not have stood a chance of being on the books of any European or North American modelling agency. One billboard, advertising a brand of jeans, showed a young woman with her back to the camera. She was coyly smiling over her shoulder, displaying her jeans-clad behind in all its full and round glory. I caught Marcus staring at the billboard. Unabashed, he whistled. He quite clearly preferred a fuller, voluptuous figure on a woman.

As we headed into the city, I realised that Nicaragua was growing on me. I liked the metal trees and I liked seeing the revolutionary memorabilia everywhere. The best example was a huge billboard of former activist, Hugo Chavez, standing proudly in the middle of a roundabout. His depiction was the classic one: green military uniform, red beret and stern expression. He was, of course, surrounded by metal trees. Further along the same road was a large bronze statue. It showed a bare-chested revolutionary hero pointing an automatic weapon into the sky. It looked like the type of thing found in Russia or Mozambique.

In the centre of the city were some of Managua's grandest buildings. One was the National Palace, a white-columned edifice that was so large and Greek-looking that its name fitted the bill perfectly. Built in the 1930s, the palace formed one edge of Plaza de la Revolucion. During the 1972 earthquake, it had somehow remained standing while other structures around it cracked and buckled. Twenty years after the revolution, it became the museum it is today.

Opposite the palace stands the old cathedral. Built in the 1930s, it too remained standing after the earthquake. Maybe God had saved it, some had suggested in the aftermath of the quake. But investigations proved otherwise. The cathedral was in such a precarious state that engineers condemned it immediately, banning anyone from entering its premises. And that is how the old cathedral has remained ever since.

From a distance, the cathedral looked fine and dandy. Sure, it seemed like it could do with a spruce up, but apart from that, perhaps due to its girth, it was still an impressive sight. Upon closer inspection, however, a truer picture was offered. For a start, there were no windows or glass. The interior was bare concrete. Large yawning cracks crisscrossed the stonework, some of them many metres long. One of the bell towers was listing at a hazardous angle, with its stone cross toppled pathetically across the dome. And though I might have been mistaken, it looked like a few bullet holes covered the front façade.

But why was it still standing? After all, no one could enter and use the cathedral. Was it there to remind people about the earthquake? I doubted it. In fact, should another earthquake occur in Managua, it would surely come crashing down. I was pondering this when Marcus approached after having finished his latest smoke. I asked him why it hadn't been pulled down.

"I'm not sure. But recently there has been some work going on. Maybe they think it's safe now. Who knows?"

"What work have they done?"

"If you look near the top, you can see some restoration. It's lighter brown."

I stared up and could see what he meant. But it was hardly restoration work; it looked more like superficial plasterwork than deep structural engineering works. It was like sticking a plaster over open-heart surgery.

9

Marcus wanted to show me something unusual. When I pressed him for clues, he told me to wait and see. I smiled, wondering what it could be, marvelling at Marcus' change of mood since I had first met him at the airport. Yes, he still liked cracking his knuckles, and he still had a terrible habit of tunelessly singing along to old eighties pop hits, but he had turned into a nice guy.

After a short drive, passing more Trees of Life (one of which was lying horizontally by the side of the road awaiting its 'planting'), we turned into what looked like another park. A sign told us we had to pay to proceed, but somehow Marcus charmed the woman in charge into letting us in free.

"See what I mean," said Marcus as we strolled through the miniature town. As tall as monsters, we towered above the buildings of Managua, carefully recreated in the form of scale models. There were the old cathedral, the hotels, some petrol stations and even a store advertising Hotpoint appliances. It looked the sort of place young children might enjoy, but we were the only people there, apart from a female security guard drinking a cup of coffee. Despite the lack of people, there was noise coming from behind us. The screams and shouts from a nearby open-air swimming pool and a decommissioned passenger jet showed which entertainment the people of Managua preferred. We left the park and had a look. On the side of the old Boeing 737, someone had painted *Cristiana, Socialista, Solidaria,* a strange revolutionary message to have in a children's playground, I thought. Of course the children of Managua didn't care about such things and were merrily trooping in and out, or looking towards the swimming pool and ice-cream stands. As for Marcus and me, we left the miniature town and headed to a wall overlooking Lake Managua. I tensed my nostrils in preparation for the odour, but none came. The lake and the air around it smelled perfectly normal. It looked okay, too: just a regular lake. I asked Marcus whether he'd ever been in the lake.

"In a boat, yes; swimming, no. I don't want to end up in hospital."

Close by was the mother lode of metal trees. A line of them, a forest even. They stood lined up along the lake, patrolled by a team of heavily-armed police officers. Up and down, in and around the twenty or so giant trees they walked, keeping an eye out for something or someone up to no good. That person seemed to be me. With Marcus having another cigarette by his car, I was wandering alone in the steel forest, garnering suspicious looks. But no one stopped me from taking photos or circling the trees.

An hour later, safely ensconced inside my hotel, I read a warning about earthquakes. The leaflet told me that Managua was located in an area of seismic activity and, should an earthquake occur, I would be well-advised to stay away from the window. It had a plan of my room and suggested the safest place to ride out the quake was where the red dot was. My leaflet had no red dot and therefore I could only surmise that there were no safe places. 'Once the first tremor has stopped,' the leaflet instructed, 'evacuate immediately by walking quickly and not running.'

When darkness descended over the Nicaraguan capital, I headed outside to see the metal trees. There were a few of them on the road near my hotel. They looked spectacular: bright beacons of vivid yellow and lilac. But the street on which they sat was eerily quiet. Hardly any cars drove by and there were no people. At night, like quite a few other Central American cities, the workers left the city's central core and returned to their houses in the suburbs. Managua at night was a sparkly ghost town with metal trees for tombstones.

Even so, once back in the hotel, I felt I had visited Managua at one of the best possible times: the city was on the up, it seemed perfectly safe and, best of all, it was without the tourist masses. And it had metal trees. Which other city could boast that?

But now I had Costa Rica to look forward to. San Jose, its capital, was supposedly not much to look at, but its surrounding countryside was. And that was my plan when I got to my seventh nation of the trip: to visit some Costa Rican jungle to see some hummingbirds.

MANAGUA

Top: A Tree of Life next to a monument to Augusto Sandino, a Nicaraguan
national hero; Downtown Managua, busy with traffic and metal trees
Middle: Colourful doorway in Granada; Monument to Ruben Dario, one of
Central America's greatest poets; An old revolutionary statue in the centre of
Managua; Granada Cathedral
Bottom: The quite ugly Managua Metropolitan Cathedral; A security guard
pretends she is a giant in the miniature town

Chapter 7. San Jose, Costa Rica

FCO Travel Advice: You should maintain the same level of personal security awareness as in the UK. Avoid poorly-lit or remote areas.

My alarm awoke me at 5.30 a.m. Half an hour later, with the sun making its way over the horizon promising a nice day, I was in a taxi back to the airport. I had wanted to set off at 6.30 a.m., but the hotel staff had convinced me that getting to the airport early would be prudent and so I had set off at six. At Managua International Airport, queues and immigration took a long time, they told me the previous evening, and some people had missed their flights because of this.

The streets of Managua were busy, despite the early time. People were climbing out of minibuses or were wandering along on their way to work. Chicken buses plied the roads while smoke-spewing trucks blasted their horns at any vehicles foolish enough to get in their way. When my taxi stopped at some traffic lights, I looked along a residential street behind a tyre garage. Any gangster-movie director would be impressed with the scene: three street-corner hoodlums in puffy shorts, sleeveless T-shirts and trainers standing around looking for trouble. Except they were probably waiting for a bus to take them to university.

The lights changed and I yawned and then yawned again. The driver, a squat man of few words, set off, yawning too. When I arrived at the airport fifteen minutes later, I found a terrible queue for Copa Airlines, my carrier for the short hop to San Jose. There was little order to the queuing system, and by the time I reached the front, forty minutes had elapsed. It was a good job I had turned up so early. It was now ten past seven and my flight was due to leave at the quite precise time of 8.04am.

"I'm sorry, Mr Smart," said the check-in agent. "There is a thirty-minute delay for your flight."

I asked why.

"I'm sorry, sir, I don't know."

I nodded. They never did. But I could live with a thirty-minute delay. It would actually mean I could buy a cup of coffee to send some caffeine around my ailing system. I grabbed my boarding pass and trooped off to security.

Ten minutes later, things took a turn for the worse. The half hour delay had morphed into a four hour delay according to the board. *Four hours!* That was insane. Why was a 56-minute flight delayed so long, anyway? No one knew, certainly none of the Copa airlines staff I managed to track down. What made it even more infuriating was that another Copa Airlines flight to San Jose was about to board. Why couldn't they put some of us on that flight, or better still, stick us on a flight with another airline? There were plenty to choose from. My only full day in Costa Rica was being eroded and there was nothing I could do except silently fume.

With a departure time now of 12.40 p.m., I sat down and tried to keep calm. Five minutes later, I was pacing around the small terminal, unable to settle, watching another flight leave. And so the next few hours passed in a state of boredom mixed with a side helping of major irritation. Then things got worse.

There was announcement that my flight was delayed for a further two hours. The original 8.04 a.m. departure had mutated into a jaw-dropping time of 2.40 p.m. I huffed and I puffed and then marched off to find a Copa Airlines employee. They were hard to find, keeping themselves hidden from passengers such as me, and so I took the unprecedented step of going back through security and heading to the Copa Airlines check-in desk where one solitary employee was waiting around with nothing to do. I asked her a straightforward question: why was my flight delayed so much?

"There is a delay with the incoming flight." A standard-issue response, up there with the old favourite 'technical difficulties'.

"Okay, so how about you get me on the Avianca flight? It leaves soon."

"I'm afraid I can't do that."

"Why not?"

"Because your flight has not been cancelled, only delayed."

"Yes, but don't you think a six-and-a-half hour delay is a bit excessive?"

"I'm sorry, sir, there is nothing I can do."

It was the answer I expected but I was not about to give up without a fight. "Fine. So can I ask about compensation please? A delay of this length surely warrants some form of compensation?"

The woman shook her head. "I'm sorry; there is no compensation."

"Okay, what about a meal voucher?"

"I'm sorry…"

"Anything?"

"No."

I shook my head and walked away. Thank you, Copa Airlines. Nothing from you at all. Not even a couple of dollars to buy a drink. You're on your own. A six-and-a-half-hour delay: deal with it.

What an abysmal disaster. I could've spent longer in Managua, and maybe gone to the volcano that had been a washout the previous day, especially now that the sun was shining. I could've had an extra couple of hours in bed. Then I thought about the things I would not see in San Jose and I felt hard done by. For the next two hours I brooded and watched a pigeon. It was trapped in the terminal rafters, spending most of its time fluttering between the white ceiling beams or else walking up and down them. I knew exactly how it felt.

2

I eventually landed in San Jose at 3.30 p.m. No apologies from Copa Airlines, just a nod from the cabin crew as I exited the aircraft. Victor, the airport taxi driver, was nice though. He commiserated with my plight, telling me it wasn't fair. I moaned for a bit and then decided to shut up; I was in Costa Rica and I should at least try to enjoy what time I had available. If I was lucky, I might have a couple of hours of sightseeing before sundown.

"Your country looks like it's doing well," I said, gesturing outside at the modern highway, the new cars and the large billboards advertising everything that wealthy and upwardly mobile people might need. Perhaps it was doing so well because, unlike its neighbours to the north, Costa Rica had never suffered at the hands of a dictator. Without a lunatic at the helm, the nation had got on with establishing the longest-running democracy in Central America, helped, no doubt, by the fact it abolished its army in 1949. Instead of guns and soldiers, Costa Rica spent its money on education, security and culture instead. It was like the Switzerland of Central America.

"Yeah, we are. We're lucky; we and Panama are doing okay. That's why we get Nicaraguans coming here to find work – picking bananas and coffee, you know. Back home, their minimum wage is something like two hundred dollars a month; here it's double, maybe triple that."

"Ever been to Nicaragua?"

"No way. Too dangerous. Too many bad guys and gangs. Same with El Salvador and Honduras. There's no way I'd go to any of those places." It was the familiar refrain: people in one country wary of travelling to another.

Victor explained that San Jose did have some gangs linked to the drug trade, but nothing compared to the countries further north. "There is one area near the city centre that tourists should avoid, though. It's where people have built shacks without permission. At first, there were maybe a couple of hundred of them, but now there are thousands. And that's where you find the drugs and crime."

I asked why Costa Rica didn't have the same issues with drug gangs as its neighbours to the north.

"These gang bangers all have tattoos, right? And they have them on their faces, their necks, their arms, so if anyone turns up at the border with these tattoos, they're taken to a special room and spoken to. If the security guy thinks he's a gang banger, he's out of here – put back on the next plane to Guatemala City or San Salvador. And our guys are good at their job – they know how to flush these gang bangers out."

Because it was close to 4 p.m., the traffic was getting bad. A thick snake of vehicles was making its way into the city, inching forward, bumper to bumper. In the wait, Victor told me that life was good in Costa Rica for most people. They had a stable government, good jobs, electricity that never went off and decent opportunities for anyone who wanted to further themselves. "People can be successful here if they want it badly enough. For example, my wife is from the Dominican Republic and, before I knew her, she moved here to work as a cleaner for a rich family. She worked hard, saved her money and then, when she had enough in the bank, she paid for a college degree in pharmacy. And that's what she does now – she's a pharmacist. She earns way more than me and all because she wanted success."

We moved on to the topic of earthquakes. Victor nodded knowingly. "Let me tell you something: the most exciting event of my life was an earthquake. In 2009, I was in a hardware store in the city and I felt one. I knew it was an earthquake because we get so many here, like maybe seven per month. But this was one was a bad boy. The store started shaking and everyone ran outside; you don't want to be inside when an earthquake is happening. Man, what I saw that day will stay with me forever. The ground was moving up and down and from side to side. It was as if the road was made out of rubber or cloth or something. Trees, lampposts, street signs were all leaning around all over the place. Dogs were barking like crazy and the birds were noisy as hell. Then cars started jumping off the ground. It was unbelievable and, for maybe thirty seconds, I didn't know whether to laugh or cry. And then it stopped. Just like that. The road was back to normal – not even a crack. It was amazing, actually."

"And you get six or seven earthquakes a month?" Again, I wondered whether I would experience one while in San Jose.

"Yeah, but they're usually small ones, like maybe 3.1, 3.2 on the scale. You feel the ground go a little and it feels unusual. But the city is well built and nothing major is ever destroyed. But that earthquake I was telling you about, if it had hit somewhere like Managua or San Salvador, hundreds of buildings would have come down for sure."

As we approached the hotel in downtown San Jose, the rain started. Heavy, greasy droplets fell onto the windscreen, a precursor to the torrent about to come. And when we pulled up outside the hotel, a howling wind joined the party. That was that, I thought. With the combination of a storm raging over the Costa Rican capital and my late arrival, any chance of sightseeing was now out of the question.

3

The weather was fine the next morning and my room offered a great view of the city. San Jose was a huge, sprawling mass, spreading out in all directions until a distant line of cloud-topped mountains stopped it. Unsurprisingly, given the region's seismic activity, the vast majority of buildings were low-level and not particularly arresting to look at from afar, and so, after a quick photo, I headed downstairs to meet Gus.

Gus was a gent in his late twenties who was wearing a flat cap. He was going to drive me to La Paz Waterfalls, an area of Costa Rican natural beauty to the north of the capital and then, afterwards, drop me off at the airport so I could catch my evening flight to Panama. But first, he agreed to drive me into the city centre so I could see a few of the sights I had missed the previous day. Without a minute to spare, we set off downtown.

"Tax is the biggest problem in my country," Gus told me as we negotiated our way through the centre of San Jose. He noticed me looking at a tall residential tower block outside, easily the tallest building in the city. It was earthquake- and-hurricane-proof, which meant each apartment commanded a hefty price tag. "For the people who live there, tax is not a problem, but for the rest of us, it's hard. For example, if the government decides to build a new coastal highway, they will get engineers from Spain to design and build it. Half way through its construction, the government will realise they can't afford it, so they need to tax something. So one day you'll wake up and there'll be a new tax on shoes or milk. Whenever they need money, they invent a new tax. Take this car. I pay six hundred dollars a year just to keep it on the road." He tapped a small sticker. "This says I've paid the money. If the police see a car without one of these stickers, they'll take it away and the owner will have to pay the six hundred plus a big fine."

To me, despite the heavy taxation, the Costa Rican government looked like they were ploughing plenty of money back into the city. San Jose was easily the most modern and clean place I'd visited on my trip. In fact, I could have been in Los Angeles or Barcelona.

Ten minutes later, we managed to find a parking space near a restaurant specialising in chicken dishes. The road was Avenue 2, one of the main arterials that cut through the city in an east-west direction. Like many Central American roads, it was busy with chicken buses, taxis, cars and pedestrians. Unlike the majority mestizo populations of the countries further north, Costa Rica's citizens seemed mainly white, a holdover from the Spanish, who managed to wipe out most of the indigenous population.

Before I jumped out to take some photos, Gus told me that San Jose was perfectly safe. I could wander around the city, night or day, he told me, and take photos of whatever I wanted to without anyone bothering me. He told me to start at the cathedral and then make my way to the central park. "But let me tell you something a few tourists have told me. They say that San Jose is the ugliest capital in Central America. I don't know whether this is true, because I've only been to Panama City, but I thought I'd just warn you."

4

The Metropolitan Cathedral of San Jose was grey with green domes. Its best features were its immense size and a statue of the Pope outside. Central Park was better, featuring a gigantic domed bandstand in the centre, which was popular with the locals taking a breather from city life or with joggers stretching and lunging like exercise freaks. The bandstand looked like some sort of alien spaceship projecting thick orange laser beams from its central core; next to it, a massive Costa Rica flag billowed at the end of a pole.

I took a few photos and climbed up the bandstand, managing to avoid a flock of pigeons that flew right at me. Gus was sort of right: San Jose wasn't the prettiest place I had been to, but it certainly wasn't the ugliest. At worst, it looked a little muddled. The mishmash of structures in the park, which also included a statue and a gaudily-coloured sign saying *San Jose Lives!* made it too cluttered for my liking.

A short walk away from the park was perhaps the grandest building in the city – the post office, a monumental edifice that took up one size of a busy plaza. It looked like a presidential palace or an important governmental establishment and yet its vastness was just for posting letters and buying stamps. It was full of arched windows, fancy columns and fetching facades; I peeked inside to see a queue of people waiting for their parcels to be weighed.

"Well, what do you think?" asked Gus when I returned to the car.

"It's not as ugly as I thought, but I think I know what the problem is. In other cities, all the important and beautiful buildings are more or less in the same place. But here, they are all spread out. And there's not that many of them, either."

We drove up a slight hill where what looked like a fairy-tale castle stood at the top. Decked out in yellow and topped with red turreted columns, it looked like it was made of Lego; it was actually a children's museum, full of interactive and educational displays covering astronomy, science, the natural world and many more things besides. Queuing up outside were plenty of kids with their parents in tow. And though the Museo de los Ninos looked a place of frivolity, for seventy years between 1910 and 1979, it had been anything but, for it used to be San Jose's much-feared Central

Penitentiary. According to Gus, the conditions for the prisoners had been hellish. Rampant overcrowding, scant food supplies (often supplemented with rat meat) and daily violence were only three of the nice things on the agenda for the prisoners. Things got so bad it was closed down due to the inhumane conditions. That's when someone had the great idea of ripping out the cells and installing some child-friendly displays.

Not far from the former prison was a district of San Jose that Gus told me was one of the most dangerous. "This is where the bad guys live," he said, as we came to a standstill at some traffic lights. Opposite us, huddled around a black lamppost littered with old flyers, was a group of seven or eight young men with seemingly nothing better to do than to hang around and look menacing. Half of them favoured baseball caps. All looked like extras for *Breaking Bad*.

"At night, these guys will rob you, no question. And if you manage to escape them, then the prostitutes and homeless people will get you."

I could already see a few of the city's homeless. As we drove through the neighbourhood, passing run-down stores and vehicle repair shops, the vagrants were still asleep. How they could snooze with the honking traffic I did not know. One person was awake, though: an old man with days-old stubble and scraggly, unkempt hair. He was putting in his contact lenses with the aid of a broken shard of mirror. Beyond the road were shacks with corrugated roofing. All of them had satellite dishes.

I asked whether any tourists had ever been harmed in Costa Rica.

Gus nodded. "Look, Costa Rica is like anywhere: there are bad guys who do bad things. Though, compared to El Salvador and Honduras, our murder rate is low. But a tourist was murdered here in March. He was a Canadian on vacation with a group. He was staying in Puerto Viejo, which is over on the Caribbean coast. His guide told him not to go outside by himself, but he did. He got up early so he could take some photos of the sun rising over the beach and that's when they got him: homeless people on the beach. They saw him with his camera and thought, "I want that"; when the guy refused to hand it over, they stabbed him to death and took it anyway. And there was another tourist who got attacked by an alligator last year. But he survived, I think."

We emerged from the crime district unscathed and began a drive up and out of the valley away from the city.

5

"I can't believe you're only in Costa Rica for one day, man." We were threading our way ever so slightly upwards, passing through gorgeous green countryside. Banana and mango trees were spilling out into the road. The scenery dripped with pure Central American *tropicalness*. "But, if you're only here for a short time, then La Paz Waterfalls is the place to see."

An hour's drive from San Jose, La Paz is one of the prime tourist sites near the capital, not just for the waterfalls but for its lush tropical rainforest and wildlife. It was possible to see toucans, hummingbirds, jaguars, poison-arrow frogs and spider monkeys up close and personal. If the desire took me, I could even milk an ox.

Gus told me that an American man had founded the complex. "He was visiting Costa Rica when his guide mentioned a waterfall he might like to see. So they trudged across some weed-covered farmland until they saw it. The American was so impressed that he went to see the farmer who owned the land and bought it. Then he bought more land from the Costa Rican government until he had about seventy acres. That's when he set up the La Paz Waterfall and Peace Lodge Gardens. There's a small hotel there where the cheapest room is four hundred dollars a night."

I whistled. "So someone must be making a lot of money?"

"Oh, definitely. Especially since it costs fifty bucks to get in. But everyone says it's worth it."

We passed through Alajuela, Costa Rica's second largest city. It looked well-kept, with a fair smattering of colonial buildings in the centre. Gus stopped near the central square, pointing out a tree. Large fruit hung from its branches. "When I was ten, I was walking under that tree with my father and a mango dropped on my head. Man, it hurt! I thought my skull was cracked open."

I laughed.

"But the reason we've stopped is not because of the mango tree but because of that statue. Can you see it – the soldier holding a rifle in one hand and a flaming torch in the other? His name is Juan Santamaria." I looked and nodded. The soldier was leaning forward, the torch held out in front of him. Gus told me his story.

Juan Santamaria was born in Alajuela in 1831 and, in his infancy, developed a love of drumming. Whenever he got the chance, young Juan would bang away on pots and crates he found on his father's farm. Then he grew up and his dreams of drumming receded as he began to work as a farm hand. Aged twenty-four, things were afoot in the north. William Walker, the mad American who had somehow become President of Nicaragua, was causing a stink. When the Costa Rican president heard of Walker's plans to create a slave state, he roused the national spirit in his citizens, asking them to take up whatever arms they could and head north to fight off Walker and his cronies. This is where Santamaria's skill at percussion came to the fore, because he joined the army as a drumming soldier. It wasn't his drumming skills that earned him a place in history, though.

As Santamaria marched north into Nicaragua with his compatriots, he banged his drums and fought small skirmishes against Walker's men. One battle in particular was where Santamaria made his name. With some of Walker's men holed up in a hostel, it was decided that in order to flush them out someone should creep up and lob a burning torch through one of the hostel's open windows. It was a suicide mission, everyone knew; while people shuffled and stared at their shoes, Juan Santamaria stepped forward.

With his torch, the young drummer crept towards the hostel. As he did so, one of Walker's men spotted him and took aim. It was an easy shot for the marksman because the drummer was moving so slowly. Though mortally wounded, Santamaria still managed to throw his torch with good aim, for it disappeared through a window and set fire to the hostel. As Juan Santamaria died, Walker's men fled or were captured.

For this deed in securing a decisive victory, Santamaria became a national hero in Costa Rica, with the date of his death commemorated as a national holiday. When they built an international airport, they named it after him.

6

Gus asked whether I wanted to stop for a coffee. He told me he knew of a place en route that sold the best coffee in Costa Rica. "Plus you get to see a coffee plantation up close."

It would be good to get a cup of coffee, I thought, but not if it involved a hard sell from the proprietor in return for the thimbleful of espresso. I questioned Gus about this. "No man, it's just a regular café. You order a latte or a flat white or whatever and look out over the plantation. Sure, there is coffee to take away, but no one's gonna force you into buying it."

On the apex of a small hill was the café, with two large touring motorcycles parked outside. On the opposite side of the road was a thick grove of banana trees. An elderly man with a fearsome machete was chopping a huge bunch down. Inside the café, I ordered a latte and got an espresso for Gus. At the other end of the café were a couple of middle-aged men, both American and clearly the owners of the bikes. We all nodded at one another and then, armed with my latte, I wandered to the veranda to spy upon the coffee plantation.

It was vast, a never-ending swathe of thick, bushy green that stretched across a tree-edged valley. I took a hearty sip of my drink and concurred that Costa Rican coffee was good: enough zip to give me a caffeine boost, but more than enough flavour to duly savour. Gus joined me on the balcony, asking me what I thought of the coffee. I told him it was great.

"I was here a few weeks ago with the worst client I've ever dealt with. He and his wife were on a three-day tour of Costa Rica, but I tell you, those three days felt like a month. She was great – polite and educated – but the guy, I think he was from Azerbaijan, he was a major pain in the ass. Did nothing but complain."

"Complained about what?"

"About their hotel – the bed was uncomfortable, the breakfast horrible, the evening meal terrible. In fact, every meal they had in Costa Rica was horrible, according to him. He also moaned about the wildlife, saying that he expected to see jaguars wherever he went; when he didn't, he thought it was my fault for taking him to the wrong places. He moaned about the weather whenever it rained – in the rainy season! When I brought them here, he said the view was boring and the coffee tasted awful. He thought La Paz Waterfalls was a waste of time. At the end of the tour, he refused to pay because he said the tour was no good. His wife had to pay. A miserable guy from start to finish."

We finished our coffees and headed down the steps to the plantation. The coffee plants were about a metre high, with branches covered in clusters of green coffee fruit. Gus knelt down and held a few beans in the palm of his hand. "It's July now, and these beans will not be ready until November. That's when the fruit turns red. They produce coffee every five years or so. And these coffee plants live for maybe sixty or seventy years."

"And the coffee I just had was grown in this plantation?"

"Absolutely. From field to cup in ten metres."

7

I don't know why I expected La Paz Waterfalls to be devoid of tourists, but I was wrong. The first indication of this was the car park. It was so full to bursting that we had to park in a secondary car park which was basically a field. Then I had to queue to get inside and I counted twenty-eight people in front of me. Assuming all of them were tourists (which they had to be) almost one thousand dollars was coming through the door in about fifteen minutes. And if they had lunch, then you could add another $350. And this did not include the people behind me who were arriving in a constant stream.

"Is it always this busy?" I asked Gus.

"Always. But like I said before, it is worth the wait and the money to enter."

I nodded, feeling a little aggrieved. So far on my trip, I'd had the sights more or less to myself, but not anymore. Tourists had caught up with me big time in Costa Rica, most of them American by their accents. But then I countered my own argument; I was a tourist, too, no different from anyone else in the line.

We shuffled forward while some people in front inspected the paper wrist bands they had been given. A certain colour indicated whether they had paid for lunch or not. "So are the animals kept in cages? Like in a zoo?" I asked Gus.

"Some of them. The jaguars and big cats are. So are the monkeys and toucans. But the hummingbirds are wild, and most of the park is jungle. It's not like a zoo though, because the animals have been saved from being killed. Some of them were found with injuries and were brought here. I suppose it's more of a rehabilitation centre than a zoo."

Because I knew I would be starving by lunchtime, I paid for the entry plus lunch, handing over $56 to the courteous young woman behind the counter. She wrapped a band around my wrist, telling me this would allow me entry into the restaurant. I thanked her, wondering whether I would get my money's worth. Leaving Gus in the lobby to read a newspaper for a few hours, I stepped outside. And then a hummingbird whizzed past my head.

The tiny green bird fluttered around a flower and then settled on a branch, its plumage almost metallic-looking in the glorious Costa Rican sunshine. For some reason, I was the only person who had noticed it – everyone else was making their way along one of the nature trails that led around the complex. So I savoured the sight. It was tiny, with a minuscule elongated beak, which it swivelled towards me for half a second before flying away, faster than my eyes could keep up. Perhaps the entry fee was worth it after all.

For the next few hours, I wandered around all the enclosures, seeing toucans, parrots, ducks, brightly-coloured finches, monkeys, butterflies and monkeys. But I could not ignore the fact that things seemed very zoo-like. True, the enclosures were larger than most zoo cages, and they were decked out with authentic-looking jungle scenes, but the animals were still essentially trapped, unable to freely move about as they could in the wild. And people were everywhere, sticking their cameras up to the glass or through the fencing. It all felt a bit forced.

A small clearing provided a better experience. Small circular birdfeeders hung from branches and all were busy with the rapid flutter of tiny wings. Every few seconds, a hummingbird would whiz past my face, momentarily sounding like a handheld fan against my ear, so it could hover by the feeder. I was inches from them, watching with fascination as their tiny tongues darted in and out, wings beating as much as eighty times every second. To the human eye, it was as if a shadow surrounded the bird's body.

I wandered into another covered enclosure supposedly teeming with frogs. I saw some in glass cages, but despite the presence of luxurious vegetation and ample ponds, I could not for the life of me find one.

A couple of Germans came in behind me. They looked around for a few moments and said something to me, which was probably: *there are no frogs in here; we're off to see the jaguars*. I nodded and smiled but hung around for more amphibious detection work. I pored over the pond, studied some leaves (even their undersides) and diligently checked all the rocks but, unless the frogs were all under the surface of the pond, the whole place was devoid of frogs. I checked another stone in case one was camouflaged upon its surface. Nothing. And just as I was about to give up, I glanced at some large leaves in the middle of the enclosure. And there one was: a tiny green frog with black spots. It was smaller than my fingernail, and utterly beautiful. When I knelt to get a closer look, I spotted a second frog, about the same size but even more vivid with a bright-red body and blue legs. It was sitting innocently in the curl of long leaf. The frog was so nonchalant that it allowed me to put my camera up close to get a photo. It was easily the most beautiful frog I'd ever seen. Later I found out it was a strawberry poison-arrow frog.

Luckily, poison-arrow frogs bred in captivity have low levels of toxins on their skin because they don't eat the same type of insects as their wild cousins. But at the time, not even aware it was a poison-arrow frog, I lightly touched my finger on it to demonstrate its size for a photo. If I had been doing the same thing in the rainforests of Colombia, home to the most poisonous variety of poison-arrow frog, I might be dead. The poison from one tiny frog's skin had enough toxicity to kill twenty people, which was why local tribesmen famously used it to coat their hunting arrows.

After the fun of the frogs, I had some lunch and then moved to the star attraction – the big cats. The ocelot enclosure contained three small, but beautifully spotted, jungle cats. They were so striking (and less threat-inducing than the bigger jaguars) that I could see why Salvador Dali had kept one as a pet. One was asleep but the other two were climbing along a wooden branch. A small notice informed me that the cats were too old, injured or reliant on human help to ever be released back into the wild.

The jaguars were huge and menacing. This majestic big cat's bite was the strongest of any feline, twice as powerful as a lion's. Its favoured kill method was to chomp on the back of a victim's head and crush the skull. The jaguar I was looking at was yawning, flashing its huge canines at me and a trio of Japanese tourists.

Across Costa Rica, and the region as a whole, jaguars are a threatened species, mainly due to loss of habitat and the fact that farmers kill them. During the 1950s, it is estimated that around 350,000 of these big cats roamed around, their habitat stretching from the southern United States all the way down to Argentina. Then poachers set about killing them for their fur, skinning over ten thousand a year during the 1960s and 1970s. Nowadays, the fur trade has ceased but only around 15,000 jaguars remain in the wild. In Costa Rica, when a poor rancher loses a cow, he wants to protect his herd and the easiest way is to shoot the culprit. It is a big problem for conservationists. They have their work cut out educating the farmers that trapping a cat is a viable alternative to shooting it dead. But the message is slowly getting through. In 2014, this exact scenario played out for one Costa Rican beef farmer. He went in search of a missing calf and discovered it dead, covered in blood with a large chunk of its chest missing. It was a classic jaguar kill. Instead of reaching for his shotgun, he called in the experts who set a trap, knowing the cat would return to the kill after dark. Which was exactly what happened. The jaguar was captured, transported to an area well away from farmland and released.

I looked at my watch and realised that, somehow, I'd been looking at wildlife for close to three hours and I hadn't seen any of the five waterfalls yet. Due to the great number of signposts, I followed a trail that took me through dense rainforest. Joining me on every step were jungle whistles, chirps, squeaks and the occasional calls from distant howler monkeys. Then another noise took over the bestial din, one much louder: a mighty cataract. I rounded a bend and arrived at a lonely platform perched above a river. To my left was the waterfall and, due to the rainy season, the gushing torrent was pleasingly thorough, roaring over the hard rock cliff at immense speed before crashing into the pool below. Spray coated my face and arms, cooling me from the tropical heat. By some strange chance, I found myself the only person enjoying the spectacle.

I left the cataract and then found another further along. It wasn't as spectacular, but just as forceful. Despite the racket from the flume, the setting was incredibly peaceful: just me, a virgin river and waterfall, all surrounded by primeval green.

Because the trail ended at a point so far removed from La Paz's main entrance, the owners has thoughtfully provided a bus to transport weary walkers back, and I was pleased to discover it was a chicken bus. I climbed aboard and found a seat near the back, savouring the smell of diesel and old leather. When it was half-full, the driver clattered it into life just as the rain began. Splatters covered the windscreen and outside the road turned into a shallow river. I smiled to myself; I had timed my visit to La Paz to perfection.

8

An hour and a half later I was sitting in the airport departure lounge. My flight to Panama City was with Copa Airlines again and I was hoping for none of the shenanigans of the previous day. With a cup of Costa Rican coffee in my hand, I found some wi-fi and left a scathing review about their shoddy service. That done, I felt better until I happened to check my credit card statement. In the space of twenty-four hours, almost three thousand pounds had been taken from it, starting off with small amounts of around £40, until the thieves were taking £500 at a time. And the thieves were the Nicaraguan tour company I had used. I couldn't believe it, but had the presence of mind to ring my credit card company to report the activity. The young man on the other end of the phone agreed with my conclusion of fraud and blocked my card immediately, reassuring me that I would not be liable for the deducted money. Then I emailed the tour company and reported the matter to them. To their credit, the owner replied straight away, telling me that he knew nothing about it, but promised to look into things. Which is what he did. He soon contacted me again, informing me that a renegade member of his finance department was responsible and the matter had been reported to the police.

As for me, brooding in the departure lounge, I waited for my heart to calm down to manageable levels and then I sought out the airport bar to buy myself a proper drink. My trip was nearing the final furlong, I realised. It was almost time to leave Central America and head back to the Caribbean.

SAN JOSE
Top: Evening closes in over downtown San Jose; Statue of Juan Santamaria,
drummer turned hero; A gorgeous little hummingbird in La Paz Waterfalls
Middle: The wildlife of Costa Rica: a poison-arrow frog, a toucan and a jaguar
Bottom: San Jose Central Post Office; A local man sizes me up; coffee beans
growing on a Costa Rican terrace

Chapter 8. Montego Bay, Jamaica

FCO Travel Advice: Crime levels are high. Gang violence and shootings are common. The motive for most attacks on tourists is robbery.

My time in Panama City amounted to only one night sleeping in an airport hotel. I didn't mind too much because I had visited the country a few years before with my wife. We had seen the canal, visited the old colonial district and I had purchased a Panama hat which I had never worn since.

The next morning I was back at the airport, pleased to find that Copa Airlines had delayed my flight by only thirty minutes this time. Two hours later, I was in Jamaica, home of reggae, rum and jerk spice. At some point in my eight-hour layover, I intended to experience them all in one way or another. But Norman Stanley International Airport had other ideas.

It was 11 a.m., and a couple of American passenger jets together with a British charter flight had landed at the same time. The airport was a chaos of shambolic queuing and cursing, most of the latter from me. The worst queue was the one for yellow fever checks. Because I had arrived from Panama, a nation rampant with mosquitoes, a nurse was required to give me the once over.

There was only one nurse and the queue was massive. With around eighty-five people in front of me, I timed how long it took her to process one passenger. The answer was eight minutes. Why it took eight minutes was a mystery since, as far as I could tell, the process only involved the nurse checking a person's yellow fever certificate and asking a few questions. There were certainly no thermometers or stethoscopes involved. I timed the next passenger – eight minutes again. With 83 people still to go, that meant that I would be waiting in the queue for eleven hours. Which clearly meant something was going wrong.

Another flight from Central America arrived and when its passengers were directed to the back of our queue, things kicked off. A large American man wearing a suit was not happy in the slightest. His wait would be about two days. "Come on," he bellowed at an airport employee. "I can't wait in that again. I was there three hours last time." He shook his head and exhaled. "Look, I haven't got yellow fever. I can promise you that. Just let me go to immigration."

The airport employee smiled but told him he had to join the queue. The man stood his ground. A small crowd gathered and were adding that they didn't want to join the queue either, and why was it taking so long anyway? It was a good question, especially since the nurse was now chatting to a security official. They seemed to be sharing a joke or something. A circus was running the airport and the person in charge was the chief clown.

But then three more nurses arrived and suddenly other queues opened. Astonishingly, I found myself at the head of one. I whooped with joy but then cursed when a woman in a wheelchair was pushed in front of me. The large American man was nowhere to be seen, perhaps on his way to a cell. As for me, I waited for the wheelchair-bound woman to be cleared of yellow fever and then stepped forward for my turn at the counter of misery.

"Where've you come from?" barked the nurse, without even looking up.

"Panama."

"Been anywhere else in the last week?"

"Costa Rica and Nicaragua."

The nurse carefully wrote all this down on a piece of paper in a neat cursive script. "Anywhere else?"

"No," I lied. There was no way she could check. Besides, there was no more room for her to write any more countries.

Finally she looked up. "You have a yellow fever certificate?"

I nodded and passed over the little yellow booklet. She found the page with all the details and ever-so-carefully copied it down onto her form. This was what the delay was: the copious copying of dates, vaccine numbers and my name. It was a pointless task, and she had to repeat it all on a separate slip of paper. One she filed away and the other she left in front of her. After doing this, she checked every detail again and then asked me a direct question. "Do you have any fever?"

"No."

"Any headache, cough or sore throat?"

"No," I lied, my head aching from the pointlessness of the questions. *But I have got Shagger's disease; I was up all night with it,* I wanted to say, but I kept quiet; if I had yellow fever or Chagas disease, I was hardly likely to admit it to the nurse. Not unless I wanted to spend the night in a hospital prison with the American guy.

"Any symptoms that could be the start of a cold?"

My nose was blocked to hell, my sinuses were playing up and I felt like I had a fever but I was not going to tell this woman that either. "No, I'm fine," I sniffled.

The nurse stared at me, assessed my wellbeing and stamped something on the form and passed it to me. "Show that to immigration."

And that was it: an utterly pointless waste of time that served no purpose except to tick a few boxes. I clearly had a cold (that might have been yellow fever, as far as the nurse was concerned) and yet I was allowed to proceed. The pointlessness of it reminded me of a time when I was living in Qatar and a famous US actor had been performing the title role in 'Richard III'. Somehow my wife had persuaded me that it would be a good idea to watch it. As a precaution against would-be suicide bombers, the security officials in the Qatari theatre had installed some metal detectors for everyone to pass through. This was all well and good for the first twenty minutes, but when announcements came over the in-house intercom system for everyone to take their seats, all hell was let loose. People were shouting for things to speed up and security officials didn't know what to do. Then someone decided the simplest solution was for the metal detectors to be switched off. The crowd surged past the security guards to take their seats. Which was why it reminded me of the yellow fever debacle in Jamaica. Either do it properly or don't waste everyone's time and pretend.

2

With forty minutes to wait for my tour guide to arrive (he was running late), I relocated to a small airport café. Its outdoor seating area was chock-full of European holidaymakers drinking Red Stripe lager or stuffing their faces on some type of baked pasty. Because it was lunchtime, I decided to buy something to eat, too. The only fodder on offer was something called a beef patty, which I bought, along with a Red Stripe. I took them to a table around the other side from the masses.

I wasn't expecting much from the cheap beef patty but when I took a bite I discovered it was the tastiest thing I'd eaten on the entire trip. It was spicy and juicy, full of beef; I wolfed it down.

"Hey man, I'm Joe," said a man's voice. I turned to see a wiry gent of about fifty wearing a thin, dirty yellow T-shirt that covered the top of his equally grubby jeans. "I've not eaten since yesterday. I've also just been in hospital." He lifted his T-shirt to show me a long, angry-looking scar, about four inches long. His eyes scanned the vicinity, keeping a practised eye out for any approaching café staff who might shoo him away.

I commiserated. "That's bad."

"Yeah..." He waited for me to offer some money and when I didn't he lowered his T-shirt. "I'm starving, man. You got something for Joe?"

"I'm sorry. I haven't got any Jamaican money, and I've just spent my last US dollars on my Red Stripe." This was partly true; there was no way I was going to give him the hundred-dollar bill I had in my wallet.

"You rich tourists are all the same." Joe sighed and sloped off towards the road that led to the departure terminal. A car trundled towards him and Joe stuck his arm out, pretending to be an airport employee. The driver stopped and after some discussion through the driver's window, Joe pointed a few hundred metres along the road, pointing in the direction in which the car had already been going. A banknote passed through the window and Joe slapped the side of the car good naturedly as it drove away. That's when I noticed two young men entering the quiet part of the café I was sitting in.

Both men looked at me and then one walked past and stood at the corner where he had a good view of both sections of the café. His pal remained by the side entrance, meaning I was in the middle. When I turned back to him, he looked away. Sitting with my small luggage, camera and wallet, I suddenly had a feeling that something was amiss and I had to act. I left my drink, gathered my things and stood. The man by the entrance looked like he was going to say something, but I was already moving into the busy part of the café, brushing past the second man. Amid the safety of numbers, I noticed both men standing together now. After a few moments, they departed whence they came.

3

Courteney was a sixty-something gent with a bald head and thick white beard. His accent sounded pure Jamaican. "Alright, man. Welcome to Montego Bay. You've come on a hot day, my friend."

I told Courtney about the men in the café.

"I don't tink they were going to steal your stuff; too many police around the airport, man. I tink they was lookin' for someone – maybe offering a taxi or tour."

I climbed into Courteney's van and we set off. Beyond the perimeter of Sangster International Airport (if only the S was a G, I thought) was a long straight road. Although the ocean was on the left, I couldn't see any sign of it, due to the proliferation of high-end hotels blocking the view. Sandals, Half Moon Resort, The Hyatt and Hilton had supersized, all-inclusive resorts along the northern coast, each with its own private beach. If I had chosen to stay at the Hyatt, it would have cost me over $700 for a single night in the cheapest room. Most of the guests who stayed in such hotels would never leave their resort for the duration of their stay. Jamaica was simply too dangerous, many people believed, for frivolous sightseeing jaunts.

I asked if Courteney ever dropped people off at the Hilton.

"Oh yeah, man. I do it all the time. And it sure looks good in there. Total luxury, you know. Why, you thinking of checkin' in?"

I laughed. "I don't think so. If I was stopping the night, I think I'd be staying over there." I pointed to some shacks on the other side of the road.

"Those houses don't look like much, do they? But they are slowly being improved. The government pays for some upgrading and the people pay the rest. Instead of wood, they might get concrete. So this means in a hurricane the house will stay up instead of ending up in the ocean." I looked at the houses a little more closely. Some of them did indeed have grey sheets of concrete supporting their corrugated metal roofs. But if this was what they looked like after improvements, God only knew what they had looked like beforehand. Then, before I could study them further, they were gone, replaced by undulating green hills. Our first stop of the tour was located up one of the hills, a large Georgian mansion called Rose Hall. Built in the late eighteenth century, it had been the home of a British slave owner. It was supposedly haunted.

4

Slaves used to be big business in Jamaica. When sugar production turned into a major money spinner for the British Empire, ships brought hundreds of thousands of slaves in from West Africa and deposited them on the shores of Jamaica. The hardship they endured on the crossing was inhuman. That was if they even arrived; many ended up at the bottom of the ocean. Take the following dreadful account of just one ship that set sail from the coast of West Africa in September 1781.

At the start of the voyage, 440 slaves were shackled and chained in preparation for the three-month crossing to Jamaica. At the halfway point, following an inspection of the human cargo, the captain decided that some of the slaves were either too ill or diseased to carry on, and so 133 of them were dragged from the slave deck and shackled together by the ankles. Then the chains were weighed down with cannon balls and the whole group was thrown overboard. Just like that: gone to the ocean without any thought or guilt. When the ship eventually arrived in Jamaica in December of that year, less than half of the original number remained, the rest thrown overboard along the way. There was uproar at this when news got out, but not because of the loss of human life, but because the ship's insurance company refused to pay for the loss of 'goods'.

At Rose Hall, around two thousand slaves worked in the sugar plantations, and their typical day involved twelve to eighteen hours of punishing labour, punctuated by whippings, beatings and sometimes death for committing the most minor of offences. Presiding over them was a British lady called Annie Palmer (though there are many questions about whether she was a real person).

Annie Palmer, born of British stock, lived the early part of her life in Haiti. When her parents died from yellow fever, she was allegedly raised by her Haitian nanny who, well-versed in the art of voodoo, began to teach young Annie her dark ways.

As she progressed through her teenage years, Annie bloomed in beauty but felt constrained by the bounds of Haiti, and so jumped aboard a ship bound for Jamaica in search of a husband. More or less as soon as she tottered onto dry land, suitors hounded her. The winner was a young man called John Palmer, owner of Rose Hall. They were soon wed and, once safely ensconced inside the vast mansion, Annie grew bored of married life and began staring at the lithe slaves who worked the grounds. With her husband always busy, Annie took things a step further and bedded some slaves. When her husband discovered the mischief, he beat her, leaving Annie battered and bitter. She was so angry she decided to kill him, poisoning him to death, telling the local constabulary that he had perished from yellow fever. Without any way to investigate otherwise, the police believed her story and she inherited the estate.

Without a husband, Annie was free to pick the strongest slaves to join her in her private chamber. Whoever was chosen went with mixed feelings. Yes, Annie Palmer was young and beautiful, but she had a terrible temper towards those who annoyed her, especially when they displeased her between the sheets. Barely a day passed without Annie ordering someone to whip a slave. Often she watched these whippings, smiling as the pain was meted out.

Then a European man came knocking at her door. He was good looking and seemed kind, so Annie fluttered her pretty eyelashes until he asked her to marry him. After they were wed, the couple lived together in Rose Hall but, behind his back, Annie could not help but take more slave lovers to bed. With kitchen hands whispering and servants giving knowing looks, Annie's second husband discovered her dalliances. Like his predecessor, he was mad as hell and gave his new wife a beating. In return, Annie stabbed him in the chest and poured hot oil in his ears to make sure he was dead. When the police arrived and asked what he hell had happened, Annie claimed yellow fever had taken him. The police looked at the bloodied chest and the congealed wax around the poor fellow's ear and nodded. Yellow fever it was.

It was at this point that Annie upped her cruelty to her slaves, enjoying their torment as she watched their whippings from her balcony. For this, she became known as the White Witch. Still young and beautiful, though, Annie married for a third time, all the while taking slave lovers on the sly. When she tired of husband number three, she enlisted the help of one of her favoured slaves to murder him. Together the pair strangled the poor man to death and then, possibly because Annie was aware that the yellow fever excuse was running a bit thin, she ordered another gang of slaves to wrap the body and bury it in an unmarked grave by the ocean. This they did, unaware that another gang of Annie's slaves were hiding in wait for them. After the first group had buried the body and made their way back to the hall, the second group sprung out and killed them. By doing this, Annie had removed all witnesses to the murder.

Annie Palmer got her comeuppance, though. In the dead of night, one of her slave lovers strangled her, finally ending her reign of tyranny. In nine years, she had seen off three husbands and hundreds of slaves. But, allegedly, ever since the night of her murder, the ghost of Annie has roamed the grounds of Rose Hall. Sometimes ghastly screams are heard in the dead of night. And because of the ghostly goings on, séances are frequently held in Rose Hall. The building has also featured on a TV program called the *Scariest Places on Earth* where an ordinary family were filmed staying in the hall for an evening of reality TV terror. They survived the night. Country & Western star, Johnny Cash, when he heard about the White Witch of Rose Hall, wrote a song called *The Ballad of Annie Palmer*.

5

Courteney pulled up outside the great hall's visitor centre. As well as the ticket office, there was a shop selling tourist knickknacks, none of which I was interested in. But because we were so high up the hill, I finally caught my first glimpse of the sea, a gorgeous wedge of blue that ran across the horizon. At the ticket office, my arrival seemed unexpected, but a guide was summoned from within. Five minutes later, a young woman appeared and introduced herself as Shauna.

While Courteney sat on a chair in the shade, Shauna led me along a pretty little path until we were standing directly in front of the great house. It looked impressive, with three storeys of white-and-grey stonework. Shauna told me that there was a fourth floor underground, which used to be the dungeons. "If a slave tried escapin'," she told me, "traps in the fields would catch him and break his ankles. The slave master would bring him back to Rose Hall and toss him into the dungeon, all bleeding and screaming, like. Annie Palmer loved hearin' those screams."

I nodded thoughtfully, even though I knew that any stories about Annie Palmer were probably fabricated, most likely taken from a 1929 novel entitled The *White Witch of Rosehall*. "Is the dungeon still there?"

"No. It's a bar now, and a storage place."

The interior of Rose Hall was pretty much what I expected: fancy chandeliers, long dining tables, paintings of unknown people, old dinner plates and expensive-looking curtains. Shauna told me that Johnny Cash had donated a lot of the items thirty years previously. "He bought a house close to here. I think he lived there until the 1980s. He left when some bad men broke into his house and took his boy hostage. He paid the ransom, got his boy back and left Montego Bay."

Upstairs were the bedrooms, all decorated period-style with four-poster beds, bed pans and rocking chairs. To get to them, Shauna and I crossed creaky wooden floorboards. At night, if a rat scurried across them, it might sound like a ghost. Shauna led me around each of the four bedrooms, telling me what had happened in each one. "This was where Annie murdered her first husband," she told me, pointing at the bed. I then proceeded to get the full and rich sordid account of the woman and her slave-loving antics. It was useful having four bedrooms, I realised, for it gave Shauna's narrative a pleasing chronological flourish. Each room was the site of another murder according to my guide, each bed the scene of the actual crime.

Down in the dungeon, a few tools and implements were on display. One of them was a hellish contraption with jagged metal teeth that would clamp together if stepped upon. Shauna asked me if I knew what it was.

"A trap?"

"Exactly, but Jamaica does not have bears and never has, so what do you think it was used to catch?"

It was hardly a question to test my intelligence. We were in a slave house, sometimes they escaped, and Shauna had already told me that the slave masters used to plant traps in the fields to catch them. "Ostriches?"

"Ostriches? We don't have ostriches in Jamaica. It was to catch slaves. And here's something else you might not know: whenever Annie's slaves were working in the house, maybe cooking or serving food, they had to whistle. If any of them stopped whistling, Annie would think they were eating some food and she would have them killed. So that's where the phrase, 'whistle while you work' comes from."

We walked through the bar area (devoid of customers) and walked back into the startlingly bright sunshine. Around the side of Rose Hall was a single, domed grave made of stone. "This is where the White Witch is buried," Shauna told me ominously. Apart from a painted white cross, the grave was bare. It made me wonder whether it was a prop. "If we are quiet, the ghost of Annie Palmer might appear. This is her favourite place…"

Both of us stood still for a moment. No ghosts appeared and the grave did not stir. While I considered when it would be okay to move again, some singing started. Instead of emanating from an eighteenth century apparition, it was Shauna singing the Johnny Cash song. Her voice was astonishingly good, offering just the correct amount of melody mixed with melancholy; in fact, it was haunting.

The lyrics talked about Jamaica from a long time ago, and then described a nice scene with Rose Hall as the centrepiece. Tomatoes were growing, as was sugar cane; then things turned sinister with the arrival of Annie Palmer, the mistress of the house. She liked some of the slaves but not others, and she liked killing her husbands, whom she buried under some palm trees. The final verses talked about her Annie's ghost roaming the estate but then ended on a positive note about people now being able to visit the house.

When Shauna finished, I clapped. If I had been a judge on X-Factor, she would've gone through to the next level.

6

Not far from Rose Hall is an area called Ironshore, one of the most affluent places in Montego Bay, where houses sold for up to half a million US dollars. As Courteney drove us through the hillside district, I could see the expensive homes for myself: huge villas with private driveways, finely-pruned fruit trees and plenty of fencing to keep the riffraff out. Ironshore looked like somewhere upmarket in Spain or Italy.

Opposite one of the houses was an old sugar mill. A tall stone cone stood amid the overgrowth, its top section sprouting saplings and bushes. Whether they were growing from the inside or had taken root on the top, I couldn't tell. The structure looked like an abandoned windmill without the sails. If I could have gone back in time two hundred years, I would have seen slaves toiling under a relentless Jamaican sun while their white masters sipped on rum cocktails from the shade of their verandas.

I asked Courteney what sort of people could afford to live in Ironshore. "Lawyers, doctors, politicians, people like that. But maybe some who have made their money from criminal activities. There are a few lottery scams in Jamaica – I think it's similar to what the Nigerians do over in Europe – but here in Jamaica, they target Americans. They tell people they have won a pile of money on the lottery but a fee is needed to release the cash. People send money to these fraudsters and the guys get rich. Some of the lottery criminals live here in Ironshore."

Later, I read that other criminals were resident in Ironshore. These unsavoury lodgers had moved into vacant houses because the real owners had either left the country or gone to prison. The article included a great quote from one disgruntled resident, written in great dialect: "Dese criminals teck ova di house den rent tem to prostitutes."

"So where does Ironshore get its name?" I asked Courteney. To me, it conjured images of iron ore being smelted along the coastlines, or else of eighteenth century dockyards taking deliveries of iron tools.

"Because when it was a sugar plantation, living here was as hard as iron."

I nodded; that made sense.

Next, we drove through a middle-class part of the Montego Bay, home to teachers, nurses and office staff. Here, the houses were not as luxurious or as large as Ironshore, but they did have character and I could actually see residents. Some were sitting in gardens enjoying the sun; others were hanging washing or fixing cars. One man was chasing a trio of goats away from a patch of grass outside his home. Some of the houses looked unfinished and Courteney explained that Jamaican houses might take a decade or more to complete. "The owners will build the lower storey first and make sure it's all nice and liveable. Then, when they've saved up enough money, they might add another room at the side. A few years down the line and they might add an upper level. Sometimes they leave the house for their children to finish."

Further down the hill we came to a district of working class housing. Courteney told me that the government had provided each family with an identical one-floor concrete house which contained a kitchen, a bathroom and one bedroom. "But most of these homes have changed since then." He slowed down to let me take in the dwellings on either side of the road. Some had two floors, some had fancy extensions built onto the sides and almost all had covered porches. None of these additions had been part of the original government-issue housing. "In Jamaica, whenever someone has some spare cash, they put it into their home. That's what these folk are doing all the time."

On the way towards the city centre of Montego Bay, we moved down into a lower rung of social housing. Here, the houses were mostly shacks with corrugated roofing. One such hut had a scrap yard spilling out from it, with rusted car wrecks in various states of repair. A dilapidated banger had missing tyres, broken windows and a large sign affixed to its windscreen: *If you can fix this, it's yours.* On a nearby iron gate was a rather confusing message: *Phone Card Chicken Sold Here,* it read, which I assumed meant two different items. Then we passed a corner shack that doubled as a shop. Metal bars covered the window and a metal cage covered the counter, offering protection against thieves wanting to steal its wares of Salt Fish, Fry Fish and Convenience Goods.

"Okay, Jason," said Courteney, "we're about to drive through an area called Canterbury. It's where all the bad boys live. It is – how do you say – a squatter's suburb. It's a place where you cannot get out of the van. Even I would not walk around there. They get drive-by shootings a lot in Canterbury, all linked to the drug's trade."

"So is it safe for us to drive through?"

"Oh yeah, man. As long as we don't stop."

"And is it okay to take photos?"

"They can't stop us if we're moving." We cleared a thick line of trees and began a drive through Canterbury.

As expected, the housing looked slipshod and haphazard. Some shacks were perched on unsteady hillsides while others looked out onto the road. I was especially interested in the people of Canterbury, hoping to spot some in the throes of illicit activity, but the only people I saw was a woman pushing a pram and a group of youths sitting on a wall.

"If we stopped and asked these boys for directions," I asked, "what would they do?"

Courtney thought for a second or two. "They would walk up to the car, reach in and steal your camera. They might point a gun in, too. Do you want to find out?"

"Yes, please."

"I think we'll just carry on to the city centre; it's close by. In fact, a lot of thieves and pickpockets from Canterbury walk into the city to do their robbin' and stealin'. Then, when they're done, they rush back to Canterbury and hide. Away from this road, Canterbury is all dirt tracks so the police cars can't go in after them. But it used to be much worse. Fifteen years ago, there was a nine-hour gun battle here, the gangs against the police. The police won, thank God."

A minute later, we left Canterbury and hit the busy streets of the city centre.

7

Downtown Montego Bay was not pretty by any stretch of the imagination. It was an amalgamation of 1960s and 1970s architecture with a smattering of modern and faded colonial buildings mixed in. Shops spilled out onto pavements, forcing pedestrians to walk in the road. One man, sitting on a stool, was almost blocking an entire street corner with his supermarket trolley full of green bananas. A couple of women had piles of clothes laid out on the pavement near him and everyone was trying to get past them, creating a pedestrian bottleneck that caused cars to slow down too.

Sam Sharpe Square forms the unruly, chaotic and brightly coloured centre of Montego Bay. A couple of banks, the Montego Bay Civic Centre, more fruit stands and a plethora of shops form the edges of the cobbled square; the shops have names such as Chin's Haberdashery, Salmon's Colour Lab (For Photos) and The Cage: We Sell, Repair, Unlock Phones which is housed in a historically significant building, dating from 1806. The small brick structure with a pointed chimney was where the town's vagrants, drunken sailors and escaped slaves had once been locked up for the night if they had failed to adhere to the curfew.

Sam Sharpe Square is named after the leader of a famous Jamaican slave rebellion, a man who also adorns the front of the Jamaican fifty dollar banknote. And with good reason. Sam Sharpe was a literate slave who had read that many of his fellow slaves across the Americas were being granted their freedom. Mexico had just freed their slaves, as had Bolivia and Brazil. Haiti had been completely free for over two decades. He wanted the same liberty for his fellow Jamaican slaves and so told his pals that they should work as normal until the Christmas festive period ended, and then lay down their tools for good.

The year was 1831 and Sam Sharpe was only twenty seven years old. Keeping true to his word, when December 27 arrived, he laid down his work tools and asked his fellow slaves to do the same thing. He told them to keep calm and not antagonise the slave owners; it was a protest not a rebellion.

Slaves began laying down their tools, much to the consternation of the British landowners. The dispute began calmly, but quickly turned violent when the slave owners started whipping their charges back to work. Some slaves fought back and then, before Sam Sharpe could stop things escalating, there was fighting going on across almost every plantation and the slaves seemed to be gaining the upper hand. Unable to cope, the slave masters called for military assistance. With their superior weaponry, the British quickly quelled the burgeoning uprising with far more force than was necessary. Sam Sharpe's peaceful protest had turned into one of the largest and bloodiest slave uprisings the island had seen.

With dead slaves littering the island, Sam Sharpe was arrested and tried. After parading him around Montego Bay's central square, he was led to the gallows. While crowds of white slave owners jeered, Sam died in the noose. But his death (and the heavy-handed British approach to putting down the rebellion) caused ripples in British parliament. Two years later, they passed the Slavery

Abolition Act, which set in motion the end of slavery across the British Empire.

In 1975, the Jamaican government announced that Sam Sharpe was a national hero. A statue showing the great man rousing the spirits of his fellow workers was constructed in Montego Bay. I found it just along from The Cage. While the people of Montego Bay walked by with jovial conversation or lounged about doing nothing in particular, I stood staring at it. Two small boys were messing around underneath Sam's raised bronze arm. I wondered whether they knew who he was.

Close to the statue is the Montego Bay Civic Centre. It houses a museum. During colonial times, the British used the building as a fancy ballroom. Inside, I was not surprised to find myself the only patron and, after buying my ticket, I left Courteney in the dimly-lit entrance and began to browse the exhibits. It was time to learn a little of Jamaican history.

8

In 1494, when Christopher Columbus sailed his ships into a quiet Jamaican bay, he found it populated by short, squat people with copper skin and flat noses. The people lived in simple huts, Columbus noted, and hunted with stone spears, cooking in clay pots whatever they caught. Columbus's men wasted no time in enslaving the lot of them, making them work in vast sugar cane fields they had planted. Within fifty years, all of the indigenous people of Jamaica were dead, either from overwork and disease or simply because the Spanish enjoyed killing them. To replace them, slaves from West Africa were brought in.

No one lamented the loss of the indigenous population, least of all the Spanish, and the Taino people are now a sad afterthought in Jamaican history, a group of people who did not have the physical strength for hard labour. Conversely, the African slaves were much hardier, capable of toiling the fields for much longer than the Taino ever had. And so, with sugar production going well, the British came knocking and kicked out the Spanish.

Tropical disease blighted the British. They also had to contend with poisonous water, dangerous food and scurvy. Many succumbed to death, usually just after they had arrived on the island. But the British persevered, mainly due to the sugar harvest and, within twenty years, they had elevated Jamaica to one of the prize jewels in the crown of the empire. They even put up with the pirates who had made their base in the east of the island.

The buccaneers were a formidable band of marauding hard-drinkers who also fitted in some womanising when they could. They had settled in Port Royal, an ideal base because it lay just off the major shipping routes between Europe and the Americas, and was within spitting distance of some Spanish colonies. This made it a handy place for pirates to conduct their pillaging runs, especially since the British authorities abided their presence on the understanding that they would protect the port in case of Spanish attack.

At the time, Port Royal was notorious as the wickedest city in the world, with taverns, brothels and goldsmiths everywhere. One visitor to the den of debauchery was Dutch explorer, Jan van Riebeeck, who, in his missives, described seeing intoxicated pirates downing ale alongside livestock. He told of parrots quaffing beer and of the endless brawls that spilled out into the cobbled streets of Port Royal. Famously, according to another pirate legend, Edward Thatch, otherwise known as Blackbeard, met a monkey in one of Port Royal's many taverns. The buccaneer became so taken with the primate that he took it as his personal pet.

Another famous pirate who had once resided within the hotchpotch of wooden buildings that formed the centre of Port Royal was Henry Morgan. Born in Wales, he moved to the Caribbean in order to make his fortune as a privateer. His skill at attacking Spanish ships meant that his wish came true. The British authorities were so taken with Morgan that they appointed him Governor of Jamaica.

Using his newfound wealth, Morgan bought some land and turned it into a plantation. When money poured into his coffers, he grew lazy and took to drinking. Soon he was an alcoholic with yellow eyes and 'jutting stomach'. He died in 1688, aged just 53, and was buried in Port Royal. Four years later, a devastating earthquake struck the town and dislodged his grave into the sea, never to be seen again.

And that might have been that for Henry Morgan, except that, 250 years on, a business enterprise called the Seagram Company decided to manufacture a type of rum. They needed a good name for their drink, and the moniker they chose was Captain Morgan. The sticker featured a jaunty pirate who looked similar to the man of the same name. Today, Captain Morgan rum is the second-largest brand of spirits in the USA.

As for Port Royal, with two thirds of the town underwater due to the earthquake, and much of the rest in ruins, the British moved their base along the coast. Port Royal limped on for a while but, after a fire and then a hurricane, it was abandoned. Today, the area is an unloved district of Kingston, devoid of any landmarks or building that would link it back to its pirate heyday. There is talk of it being developed as a cruise ship terminal that will feature a classy hotel and a line of tourist shops. What Henry Morgan would make of that is anyone's guess.

9

The lower floor of the Montego Bay Civic Centre is dedicated to slavery. I stopped at a display showing punishments. They mainly consisted of shackling, chaining, whipping or hanging; another was walking the treadmill, which featured eight or nine slaves tied by their wrists to a wooden beam that crossed above their heads. Their feet were running along grooves on a moving wooden wheel. As well as a man whipping them, the main danger to a slave was losing their footing and breaking their ankles. The second danger was exhaustion, which resulted in the same thing. To receive this punishment, a slave might have been slacking off at work, talking too much in their own language or found stealing.

I found a large open ledger filled with slave names and the punishments meted out to them. A slave called Geo Shaw had been sentenced to death. Anne Ramsay had received one hundred lashes and a six-month prison sentence. What they had done the ledger did not say. It wasn't all doom and gloom though, for one slave called John Bell had been acquitted.

One grim illustration showed the cross-section of a slave ship. The slave deck was horrendous, people packed into every available space like spoons in a drawer, with no room to turn or stretch. How any of them survived the crossing was almost unimaginable. In the rush to populate the fields of the Americas, two million Africans died crossing the Atlantic. But plenty did survive, as a nearby notice dated from July 1769 indicated. Even though it was for a slave auction in South Carolina, it was similar to those happening in and around the ports of Jamaica.

'TO BE SOLD', the notice proclaimed. 'A CARGO of Ninety-Four Prime, Healthy NEGROES, Just Arrived from Sierra Leon.'

Another lengthy tome gave descriptions of runaway slaves and the reward offered for their capture. A 20-year-old 'mulatto' (a term describing a child born to a black slave woman but fathered by a white man) called Tom Dawson had absconded from his employer. Dawson was described as 6ft-tall with a slim build, and had run away with a 'negro boy ... about 5ft-tall'. The reward was ten pounds for Dawson's capture (worth about £670 in today's money) and one *doubloon* (a Spanish coin worth around £250 today) for the boy. Another slave, described as 'a sambo man named John' who spoke good English, had run away after being released from his chains due to illness. The reward for anyone catching him was a *pistole*, a coin equivalent to two doubloons. A young 'negro woman named Flora' together with her thirteen-month-old daughter Amelia, had absconded, much to the annoyance of her owner. In his description, Amelia's owner described the twenty-one-year old as 'artful', and therefore he offered an eight-dollar reward to the person who returned Flora to the nearest workhouse so he could reclaim her. Robin the Creole, height between 5ft-6 and 5ft-8, had a speech impediment which included a bad stutter. He was also knock-kneed and lame. Five pounds was the estate's reward for his return.

10

"So yeah, most of the people you see in Jamaica are descendants from those slaves," said Courteney, as we ambled through downtown Montego Bay. "But we have a few Chinese and Indians too. The British brought them over after the abolishment of slavery, you know. They were more like servants than slaves. Most of these shops are owned by the Chinese. The Indians run the jewellery shops."

"Are you interested in seeing your West African roots?"

"You mean going back to Ghana?"

Above me, a shop caught my eye. Its garish pink paint design and four nude manikins made sure of that. As far as I could discern, it sold clothes, so the purpose of the naked plastic ladies seemed redundant. I nodded to his question.

"No, man. It doesn't appeal to me. For a start, the flight is too expensive. I'd rather spend the money on my grandkids."

We carried on walking. Like most of central Montego Bay, the street was busy with hawkers and shoppers alike. Despite my being the only white face, no one gave me a second look. "So does everyone get on with each other in the city? No racial tension?"

"Nah, man, nothing like that. Everyone is fine. It's funny, actually; a lot of people who visit Jamaica come with a bad idea of what Jamaican people are like. I'm not talking about racism here, it's more about their reputation. Look, let me ask you a question: when people in your country imagine a typical Jamaican, what do they see?"

I didn't say anything, not really knowing how to answer.

Courteney answered it for me. "Bob Marley and reggae, maybe? Rastas? Beanie hats? Does this sound about right?"

I thought about this, wondering how carefully I should tread. We were now crossing a road near a large Courts store, a large furniture and electrical outlet popular across the Caribbean. I nodded and said, "Yeah, that's probably what a lot of people think. But they also think there's a lot of crime in Jamaica."

Courteney nodded knowingly. "Exactly! Jamaica has a bad reputation. And I think I know why. Its 'cos of the Yardies. You heard of them?"

"The Jamaican gangs."

"Right. When Jamaicans emigrated to England and America in the fifties, they should have acted like responsible citizens. Most did, but some didn't. They had a chance to leave all the crap behind, but they took their bad ways with them and formed gangs. So now you have Yardies in London, places like Brixton and Notting Hill, and up in Canada too. They give us a bad name, because people see these gangs up to no good and they think that's what all Jamaicans are like."

I didn't quite agree with his theory but nodded.

"Now there is a lot of crime in Jamaica, don't get me wrong. And we do have one of the highest murder rates in the world – not up there with those Central American drug countries – but not far off. Drugs are the main issue for this. There are parts of Kingston and Montego Bay that you want to avoid, but most people are law-abiding. I just wish the bad eggs wouldn't take their problems to places like England, that's all I'm saying."

We came to a proud grey church, regarded as Montego Bay's finest. St James Parish Church, situated along the appropriately named Church Street, had everything a good church ought to have: a stout bell tower with a clock on it, an overgrown graveyard and some towering palm trees. I stopped by one grave and began to read the huge stone slab that formed the top. Interred beneath was a man called Henry Bennett, an English slave ship captain. Bennett had died in Montego Bay on the 19th April 1801, aged just 44, from a short tropical illness which, according to the inscription, he bore with 'Christian fortitude and pious resignation'.

Inside the church I walked past the empty pews until I arrived at a large stained glass window of the crucifixion. Christ seemed to be staring at down at the altar. On an upper level to the side of him was a large set of steel drums called the Pans of Peace, which was a great name, I thought. The interior of St James was devoid of worshippers, but it did have a staircase leading up to the bell tower. When I asked Courteney if it would be okay to climb them, he shrugged. "No one's here to stop you."

The wooden staircase looked rickety at the bottom and seemed positively dangerous when I was half way up. With every step, the whole unit shook, sending dark thoughts into my brain. Its flimsy barrier didn't help either, offering little protection should one of the steps crack, but I carried on until I reached the sanctuary of a wooden floor. The floor was the home of a large bronze bell forged in London. Gingerly stepping past it, I came to a barred window and peered out. The view was not worth the effort: a dreary shopping precinct that lay opposite the bell tower. I didn't linger long and met Courteney at the bottom. It was time to see some of the beaches for which Montego Bay was famous.

11

Driving away from the centre of the city, Courteney beeped plenty of his fellow drivers. Most beeped back. "Friends of mine," he explained. "About one hundred thousand people live in Montego Bay and most of them know each other. And if, like me, you work in the service industry, you get to know plenty more. That's what I was saying earlier – most people around here are friendly, law-abiding folk and not robbers or drug runners."

We turned onto a coastal road where I caught my second glimpse of the sea. It looked as gorgeous as before: a line of pure tropical blue edged by a sliver of yellow sand. We drove near a beach that seemed deserted and I thought it might be a good place to take a photo. Courteney thought otherwise. "That beach is not safe. If there's one place – apart from Canterbury – that I wouldn't visit, then it's that beach. Drug addicts hang around there, hiding, and if they caught up with you, they'd think nothing of harming you, maybe even killing you. It's not worth the risk."

Instead, Courteney took me to a large public beach. It was packed with sun seekers roasting on the sand or noisily dunking themselves in the sea. It was the stuff of holiday brochures, but a brochure for Benidorm rather than the Seychelles. Plastic inflatables littered the sea; sloshing further out were jet-skis. I strolled along for a while, trying to maintain a steady breeze on my face to keep the heat at bay. In the end, I gave up and returned to Courteney, who had elected to wait under a large blue parasol.

"This is one of the largest public beaches around here," he told me. "There are a few smaller ones, but they are disappearing." He told me that when he was a boy, his father used to take him and his sister to many of the smaller public beaches, most of which had since gone. "The government sells them to the hotels, who build walls around them and that's it; Jamaicans can't use them."

I shook my head. "It's not fair."

"There's a little beach just along from here that one hotel has been trying to buy for years. It's only a little patch of sand, no bigger than a tennis court, but the hotel wants it for their guests. They don't care how big their private beach is already, they just want more. The government has held out so far, but I think it's just a matter of time before the price is right."

We drove along a busy thoroughfare called Gloucester Avenue, locally known as the Hip Strip. The Pork Pit, Kaptain Red Hot and

Café Tease fought for attention amid shops called the Tropical Treasure Gift House and Sunshine Souvenirs. Feeling thirsty, I asked Courteney to stop at a convenience store; when he did, we heard a commotion. It sounded like a party. And then we saw the source of the din: a large open-backed lorry full of speakers and tight-T-shirt-clad dancing girls. We watched them pass, noticing the girls were wearing identical blue tops and tiny white pants.

"They are drumming up trade for one of the nightclubs. They look like they doin' a good job," remarked Courteney. We watched as a cavalcade of motorbikes followed them. Each motorbike had a young man with a young woman pressed up behind. Each woman, I noticed, was on the heavy side, but that hadn't stopped them squeezing into baby pink or sky blue hot pants. Courteney looked at them with barely disguised glee. "Oh man, look at dem. How I wish I was thirty years younger."

After buying a bottle of water, we drove into the hills to see Montego Bay's version of the Hollywood sign. Instead of stark white lettering, Montego Bay's sign was red and appropriately spelled the words Red Stripe, the national beer. The letters were huge, perched on the hillside with sturdy metal supports. They looked down upon a gorgeous slice of Montego Bay. I noticed the sun was no longer as high on the horizon as it once was, which meant it was time to go. I had a flight to catch. It was time to say goodbye to the eighth nation of my trip.

"Well, have a good flight, my man," said Courteney as we pulled up outside the airport terminal. "Hope you enjoyed the tour of Mo' Bay."

"I did. Thanks for showing me it."

We shook hands and I stepped out of the car, grabbing my luggage. Later, sitting in the departure lounge waiting for my night flight, I realised that, like a lot of places I had visited, the warnings about Jamaica had proved unfounded. Apart from the two young guys at the airport at the start of my Jamaican stopover, I had not felt a single episode of unease. Jamaicans, as Courteney had told me, were a friendly bunch – like the man who had just served me some rum. When he discovered we shared the same first name, he had poured a little extra into my glass. "Just don't tell de boss."

And so I sipped on some Jamaican rum, thinking about the final stop on my tour of Central America and beyond. Mexico was a country I had high hopes for. Unlike its neighbours to the south, Mexico was a nation well-trodden on the tourist trail, which would hopefully offer an easy end to my trip. And what made it even better was my wife was flying over to meet me. With a rendezvous in Cancun set for the next night, I finished my drink, grabbed my luggage and headed for the gate.

MONTEGO BAY
Top: A public beach in Montego Bay; Downtown Montego Bay
Middle: Sam Sharpe – slave leader extraordinaire; Rose Hall, home of the
White Witch
Bottom: Party time for the young of Montego Bay; Panoramic view of
Jamaica's second city

Chapter 9. Cancun, Mexico

FCO Travel Advice: Most visits are trouble free. Drug related violence has increased over recent years. The Mexican government makes efforts to protect major tourist destinations.

Getting to Mexico was a pain in the neck. The most obvious routing was via Miami or Atlanta, but since I was banned from America, I had the choice of either transiting back through Panama City or northwards via Canada, which was the option I went for, due to a mixture of price and flight times. It did mean a night in a Toronto airport hotel, though, and by the time I landed in Cancun the next day, it was dark. But Angela, my wife, was already there. Her flight had landed hours before mine and she was waiting in the hotel in Playa del Carmen, a town to the south of Cancun. When I burst through the door, looking dishevelled after a few weeks of Central American adventuring, Angela screamed, flapped her arms and launched herself onto the bed. "Massive cockroach!" she yelled.

I didn't think I looked that bad, but then realised she was pointing at the floor. "Where?" I put my bag down and frantically scanned the floor.

"It's gone under the TV unit. It was massive. Oh, sorry, Jason, I know you've only just got here but you've got to get it. It's massive!"

"You keep saying." I hated cockroaches like everyone else, but I duly crouched down and inspected the underside of the dark unit. All I could see was blackness. "You sure it went under here?"

"Yes. Definitely."

While Angela continued her vigil at the edge of bed, I used my phone's inbuilt torch to shine some light under the unit. There was nothing there but I was still wary. I'd read up on these loathsome insects. Cockroaches can bite if provoked, especially when people shine bright lights at them. And when they attacked, they sometimes liked to chomp down on eyebrows.

"Can you see it?" my wife asked.

"Not yet … I'm looking…"

"Just get it. I can't sleep if it's in the room."

I was now flat down on the tiled floor. My eyes were almost at the level of the unit underside and I swished the torch this way and that. Nothing: just plug sockets and fluff. And then I saw the beast. It was looking straight at me with its terrible antennae twitching at the ready. And then three things happened almost simultaneously, all of them terrible.

Angela screamed: a piercing sound of primeval terror. That was the first thing.

Then the cockroach charged at me. In an instant, due to perspective, it was as big as a dragon. That was the second thing.

The third thing was my involuntary scream as I flew away from the unit. And then I was aware of a fourth thing: Angela laughing like a lunatic. She thought something was hilarious.

I looked at her in confusion.

"Did I scare you?"

I looked at her in more confusion.

"Did my scream scare you?" She cackled again. "Did my scream make you scared like a little girl?"

"I didn't scream because of you! I screamed because of the cockroach. It was coming right for my face. And you're right; it's massive."

Angela's face fell. "You saw it! Oh my God! I only screamed to scare you." Her eyes scanned the floor. "Where is it?"

"I don't know. It was coming straight at my face and you were screaming and so I thought you'd seen it come out. By the way, have you ever seen a cockroach coming straight for your jugular waving those hideous antennae?"

"It's there!" Angela yelped, backing away onto the bed. It was, too. It was scuttling across the floor towards the curtain, which it scaled like a mountain goat. Two seconds later it was at the top, somehow tight-roping across the top of the fabric. I was on my feet again, with shoe in hand. And that is when I discovered that cockroaches can fly. This one flew at me, glancing off my shoulder on its way towards the door. And there it scarpered, through the minuscule gap. Angela stared after it for a moment and then rushed to the bathroom. A few seconds later, she sealed the paltry door opening with a towel. Then she looked at me. "Have you missed me?"

2

Playa del Carmen town could have been a bucket-and-spade resort in Spain. The town's main thoroughfare, the imaginatively titled Fifth Avenue, was a long strip of cafés, souvenir shops, money changers, bars, nightclubs and tour operators. All of the tour operators were peddling the same things: tours to Chichen Itza, snorkelling trips, whale shark watching and a whole list of outings that included zip lining, dinner cruises and fun-filled water parks mixed with historical re-enactments.

Mexico was back to the real world of tourists. Instead of being the only Western face, I was one of thousands. Old, young, slim and fat, everyone was in Mexico browsing the tourist stores that sold sombreros, bottles of tequila, gaudy Mexican wrestling masks and skulls. "What is it with all these skulls?" asked Angela. We were standing in front of a bewildering array of them. Blue ones, yellow ones, some painted with flowers, other covered in love hearts; the patterns and colour combinations were almost endless.

"It's to do with a festival called the Day of the Dead."

"Sounds like a horror film."

In actual fact, the Day of the Dead was a special event in the Mexican calendar when families gathered to pay respect to deceased loved ones. Beginning on October 31st and lasting for two days, people attended graves, offering dead relatives their favourite food and flowers or, for children, their favourite toy. Instead of being a sombre affair, it was a celebration of the person's life. Across the whole of Mexico, people took part in the celebrations. People dressed as skeletons and danced the streets as they sipped on tequila. Others recited humorous poems about their dead relatives. Inside houses, children munched on cakes decorated with sugary bones or were given sugared skulls as gifts. The Day of the Dead is such big business that it has spread to the tourist sector, hence the skulls in Playa del Carmen.

Mexico's fixation with skulls began with the Aztecs. Their love of human sacrifice meant that skulls were permanent fixtures around their temples and shrines. Nowadays, whenever archaeologists dig around Mexico they always seem to find skulls dotted about near the excavations. Indeed, a few of weeks prior to our arrival in Cancun, archaeologists uncovered a whole rack of them beneath a Mexico City street. They were part of a grisly tower of human skulls, believed to be the heads of decapitated enemy warriors. But instead of belonging to young men of fighting age (the expected profile of a typical Aztec warrior), many of the seven-hundred-or-so skulls belonged to women and children. This has led historians to speculate if Aztec armies included women and children or if the skull rack was for something else entirely and, if so, what? Nothing like it has ever been found before.

Angela and I walked away from the skull souvenirs and stopped outside another shop. I realised it was strange being with someone else after so long being by myself. For close to three weeks, I had become used to doing what I wanted, when I wanted: stopping to take photos without thought, eating a Snickers bar instead of sitting down to breakfast, and bypassing shops I had no interest in. But here, in Playa del Carmen, I was standing outside a shop that sold shoes. Angela decided to go in while I waited by the entrance.

A middle-aged man and woman walked past. Both were heavily tattooed and clearly from the UK. The man looked bleary-eyed, as if he'd drunk too many bottles of tequila the night before, and his wife looked like she could kill someone with just a frown. "Look, I said I was sorry," the man said in a Scottish accent.

"Don't even speak to me," she sneered. The man pulled a face and elected to take her advice. Then they were gone, traipsing past a medley of men trying to flog boat tours.

Just along from the touts was a nightclub called the Blue Parrot. Six months previously, a man had tried gaining entry to this popular nightspot, but bouncers refused him. Instead of walking off, he whipped out a gun and shot them dead. Then he walked inside and began shooting there. During the panicked stampede for the exit, an 18-year-old woman from Denver was trampled to death. As the gunman fled, five people lay dead. It is believed the shooter had links to organised crime but, as yet, no one has been arrested.

Crime in Cancun is a serious concern for the authorities. Rivalry between gangs fighting for turf control has caused a recent spiral in the murder rate. Gangland executions, dismembered body parts left in bin bags and drive-by shootings are all part and parcel of a drug cartel's modus operandi in Mexico's Yucatan Peninsula. But when Angela eventually emerged from the shoe shop, the biggest crime we could see was people drinking beer at 10 a.m. or men wandering around bare-chested when they should have known better. Nobody wants to see a flabby stomach while trying to keep a pint of Mexican lager down first thing in the morning.

3

"I want to buy a wrestling mask," I said.

Angela looked at me. "Why?"

"So I can wear it. I think it'll look funny. I only want a cheap one, though."

We were still walking along Fifth Avenue with all the other tourists, jostling for position as we meandered around ditherers, gawpers and people with pushchairs. They were the worst of the bunch, stopping for no reason and causing massive logjams of people to almost trip over each other or their pushchairs. If the gangland killings filtered though, I thought, and more tourists were killed, then there would be no chance of tripping up; every shop, tour operator and restaurant along the strip would be out of business in a month. This possibly explained the number of police wandering around. Not since San Salvador had I seen such a high concentration of law enforcement personnel.

As I kept my eye out for wrestling masks, Angela and I passed a striking little church. It looked like it was made of white candy, with dollops of icing rolled to form its perfect little dome and bell tower. A tiny Greek island would have been more than happy with this church, I thought; its understated white beauty was at odds with the blatant commercialism that surrounded it. When I peered into its entrance, I was not surprised to see it empty. But what a treat everyone was missing, not particularly for the interior itself but for the view out of its main arched window. Beyond the altar and crucifix was a scene of pure tropical scrumptiousness. If the manufacturer of a new pineapple drink wished to have a small backdrop to adorn their logo, then this scene was it. Wide palms and a pure blue ocean concentrated into one magical arch was a nice little sideshow to Fifth Avenue's shops.

Back outside, Angela and I walked into the scene we had seen from the window. With a full panoramic view, it wasn't anywhere near as impressive. The beer-swilling tourists spoilt it now. But then I noticed a stall selling Mexican wrestling masks. I headed to it with Angela in tow.

Wrestling in Mexico, or Lucha Libre as it is called, became popular in the 1930s thanks to a man called Salvador Lutteroth. Lutteroth, a bespectacled gent who worked as building inspector, was out for a shindig one night when he stumbled across a crowd trying to get into a small auditorium. There was no room for them inside, and yet they still crowded the entrance. When he asked why they were queuing, he was told there was a wrestling match going on inside. With no interest in the sport, he rubbed his spectacles thoughtfully and realised that money could be made from men fighting on stage. Soon after, he handed in his notice as a building inspector and became a wrestling promoter instead.

Lutteroth hired a larger auditorium and told people about an upcoming wrestling match. In his head, if this venture was successful, then he could take it to the next level. To begin with, he booked some wrestlers, hired some security and bit his fingernails. But he needn't have worried: the auditorium was sold out. And so he moved things up a notch and, because he was a clever fellow, he decided to spice up the fighting bouts with masks.

Salvador Lutteroth was savvy enough to realise than in order for Mexico's special brand of wrestling to hit the big time, he needed a gimmick, something that fans could latch onto and immediately associate with the sport. He would have heroes and villains, characters that people could love or hate. Instead of being just a sport, Mexican wrestling could be prime entertainment. So he had a mask specially made as a test case. Unfortunately, it looked like the apparel of a sex fiend, with the eyes, nose and mouth cut out of the black leather balaclava-type mask. Yet Lutteroth liked it and somehow persuaded Corbin Massey, a thirty-year-old American wrestler, to don it. Massey was hesitant, mainly because masks were not a new thing. Back in the States, some of his wrestling pals had tried wearing masks which had resulted in booing and ridicule. But the wrestling promoter was insistent, telling the American he would give him a cool name if he wore it. And so, quite reluctantly, Corbin Massey became *The Masked Marvel*, strolling out to the ring for his next match wearing the mask. It was the first time the people of Mexico had seen such a sight.

And they loved it.

The Masked Marvel was such a hit that other wrestlers began wearing masks, and thus was born the tradition of Lucha Libre, Mexican masked wrestling.

Within a few years, Lutteroth's wrestling competitions were the hottest tickets across Mexico. Luchadores (professional masked wrestlers) became household names and Lutteroth made a fortune.

When Corbin Massey moved back to the States, other masked men took his place, all of them with better masks with bolder designs. The Masked Rat, the Blue Demon and the Golden Terror all became famous, as did a silver-masked fighter called *El Santo,* The Saint.

The Saint was a 24-year-old wrestler whose real name was Rodolfo Huerta. As his fame increased, he was careful never to reveal his identity, wearing his iconic silver mask even when flying on commercial airliners or eating in restaurants. Allegedly, he even kept his mask on at home. By the 1950s, The Saint was the most famous man in Mexico even though nobody knew what he looked like. And, as well as wrestling, The Saint had his own range of comic books and then began a successful acting career. Starring in such films as *Saint Vs the Zombies, Saint Vs the Diabolical Brain* and *Saint vs the Vampire Women*, The Saint played a superhero fighting evil creatures and criminals. During his 52-film career, he became a champion to the Mexican people, a stalwart against injustice, and his popularity never waned through the decades.

By the 1980s, The Saint had all but retired from professional wrestling due to his age and failing health. His final wrestle was in September 1982, aged sixty-four, which he won. Soon after, he was a guest on a TV chat show he pulled off his silver mask to reveal an ordinary, if rather haggard-looking, Mexican face. It was the first time anyone in Mexico, apart from his wife and children, had seen the real face of Rodolfo Huerta, apart from his wife and children. A week later he was dead from a heart attack. His funeral was one of the biggest Mexico had ever seen, with thousands lining the streets, many of them wearing silver masks. Every one of them wanted to wish a fond farewell to one of the greatest heroes the nation had ever seen. Fittingly, Rodolfo Huerta was buried in his famous mask.

4

The stallholder had a terrific array of masks for sale and he wanted to point out the best ones – the ones with the best stitching and finest material. "This is *Fishman,"* said the vendor. "Very popular mask. Eyes look like fish!" He was pointing to a green mask covered in yellow lines. The eyes looked nothing like a fish, but the mask was pleasingly vivid and ridiculous-looking, the two traits I favoured most in Mexican-mask-buying consideration. But other masks looked equally good. A purple one with green lightning flashes, a white one with scary teeth and demon eyes and a black one with gold spokes radiating like the sun from the eyes: all looked like something I wanted to own.

"How much is this one?" I pointed to a black and white mask that looked half Stormtrooper and half Gene Simmons of KISS.

"Thousand pesos. Rare mask"

That was about forty pounds. There was no way I was going to pay forty pounds for a Mexican wrestling match, even if it was modelled on the one worn by the *Black Abyss*, a popular luchador from the nineties. "Forget it," I said. "I'll give you two hundred."

The man scoffed. He actually scoffed. "Two hundred is an insult. Nine hundred."

I began to walk away, but the man shouted. "For two hundred you can buy this mask." He was holding a gold mask with blue edging. Its most distinctive feature was its pointy blue ears, as if it had been made for Spock.

"Who is it?"

"*Sin Cara*: the faceless wrestler."

I looked at Angela. "What do you think?"

"What do I think? I think you're mad."

I studied the gold and blue mask. It looked utterly ridiculous. Did I really want a Mexican wrestling mask? What would I do with it? I certainly wouldn't ever wear it in public, or even at a fancy dress party; without the whole suit it would look stupid, and the notion of me wearing a full body suit of Lycra was an image I did not want to linger upon. Still, it would be cool to own my own Mexican wrestling mask and so, without any more hesitation, I took out my wallet, fished out a couple of notes and handed them to the vendor.

Ten seconds later, I was walking towards my wife as the proud owner of a new mask.

For the remainder of the afternoon, we browsed the shops and had lunch in a popular bar called Señor Frog's. It overlooked a mesmerising stretch of the Caribbean Sea, so blue and so deliciously alluring that it looked like a Photoshopped image in a magazine. While we ate, we discussed our plans for the days ahead. Playa del Carmen town was okay for a quick browse, but little else. Neither of us wanted to sunbathe for more than a day and so we decided the day after next we would visit Chichen Itza, Mexico's prime Maya hotspot. That sorted, we finished our meal, watching the waves lap against a pristine crescent of yellow sand.

That evening, we had forgotten all about the sand and were trying to come to terms with the prices in the hotel's convenience store, the convenience being only its location. "Two hundred and seventy six pesos for a small can of Bud Lite! Are they having a laugh?"

By my side, Angela whispered, "How much is that?"

"About eleven quid! For one can of beer. In the local shops it was about thirty pesos – a tenth of the price." Even a tiny bottle of water was about three pounds. It was daylight robbery, plain and simple but, with a hotel full of guests who could not nip out and buy something locally (the hotel was miles away from anything), they could charge what they liked. Even a simple ham and cheese croissant was more than twelve pounds.

Yet inside the shop was a woman laden with goods. Four bottles of water, a couple of sandwiches and a large packet of crisps filled her basket. I could only assume that she had gold bullion about her person. As for us, we left the shop empty-handed, thankful we had bought some water earlier from the town.

The prices in the hotel restaurant were also astronomical, so much so that it was cheaper to hire a helicopter to take us back into the town and eat there. We chose an open-air rooftop restaurant called La Parrila Mexican Grill. As well as an extensive menu of tacos, steaks and fajitas, its décor featured a clump of plastic cacti and a group of jolly mariachi musicians providing flavoursome tunes backed by trumpets, guitars and theatrical foot stamping. Over a couple of beers and some good food, Angela and I sat back and soaked up the tourist hotbed of Playa del Carmen. An hour later, while the young of the town emerged from taxis in high heels and lipstick, we headed back to the hotel.

5

The Chichen Itza tour was, without doubt, the worst tour we had been on. It was supposed to begin at 7 a.m. in our hotel lobby. The guide had not shown up, and Angela and I were tired and irritable. Eventually he arrived twenty minutes late and led us to his van. It looked battered and old, and the driver looked the same. Before we set off, he checked us off on his special clipboard-held list and then jostled the rusty gear lever into action, which made a suitable noise of annoyance before relenting to engage with the interior cogs. And then we were off for part two of the adventure: the hotel pick up rigmarole.

When we had booked the trip the previous day, the man on the stall, whom I shall name the Bandit, had assured us that the Chichen Itza trip was an express one. "Two hours to get there, two hours to see the ruins and two hours back. Six hours in total," he promised. Except the Bandit had lied. What he'd neglected to inform us was that for the first hour, we would be driving around the Yucatan Peninsula picking up eleven people from three different hotels. So by the time eight thirty rolled around, and we had picked up everyone else, we still had another two hours to go before reaching Chichen Itza. Except we didn't. We had far longer.

Because the driver and all the other passengers were Spanish speakers, they could enjoy hearty chitchat. Soon the whole minibus was awash with loud conversation, forcing Angela and me to sit like unwanted guests at the front. Then the driver announced we had a scheduled stop coming up and, though we didn't know it at the time, it would be the first of many.

Stop number one was a toilet stop. Except the toilet was merely the sideshow to the tourist stalls, the food stalls and the car park full of minivans similar to ours. The place was crawling with people displaying varying shades of interest and I was getting a little bit mad. "We should've just hired a car," I whispered to Angela. "We would've been there by now. At this rate, we won't be there until at least lunchtime."

My wife nodded. "But there's nothing we can do now."

There was, I seethed. I could don my wrestling mask and put the driver in a headlock. Except I'd left the damned thing at the hotel. Eventually, at 10.30 a.m., we were all back in the van to continue the journey.

Stop number two was worse than the toilet stop. And it was only half an hour later. This time there were coaches in the car park and men dressed up in orange plumage with their faces painted as skulls. If we wanted to, we could have posed with them in exchange for some pesos; instead, we traipsed past and found a mob of people gawping downwards over the edge of a large circular cliff. Below them was a pool of water where people were swimming or waiting on ledges to jump in. The cliff and pool was a *cenote*, a limestone sinkhole, one of many such things in Yucatan, and the Spanish contingent from our minibus were making a beeline to some changing rooms so they could get in it themselves.

"What a load of rubbish," I said, huffing and puffing. "This was meant to be the express tour to the ruins so we could miss all this out. The Bandit has well and truly stitched us up. And we're here for an hour and twenty bloody minutes."

We walked around some stalls and then walked around them again. Then we tried to get into a café, but the owners barred us from entry saying we were not wearing the correct bands or something. So we found a shifty-looking bar and ordered some beers even though it was barely lunchtime. The only solace was when I zoomed in on a photo I'd taken of our guide's clipboard. It had a list of people's names, the hotel they were staying at and, most interestingly, how much they had paid for the trip.

"We paid $140," I said. "Which is well over the odds, but it's not as bad as what some of these poor buggers paid. This guy here," I said, pointing at a name that read Felipe, "has paid $160. Twenty dollars more than us." I zoomed into the lower portion of my sneaky photo and sniggered. "This one's worse. He paid $180!" I gestured around us. "One hundred and eighty dollars for this?"

Angela sipped on her beer. "But they all seem to be enjoying themselves. So who got the better deal?"

I mulled over this and then nodded miserably. "Them."

At 1.30 p.m. we took our third scheduled stop, this one for lunch. We were told to go into a large rectangular building that stood opposite a small square of souvenir shops, all selling exactly the same things: painted skulls, postcard and paintings. The best picture featured four Mexican revolutionaries sitting on the front of a Wild West steam locomotive. It dated from 1910, and all four men wore huge sombreros and carried long rifles, their stern expressions tempered by their comical hats. Whether they had just robbed the train or were merely riding on it was unclear.

The restaurant was packed, and when Angela and I moved into the right-hand section, we were immediately stopped by a woman who seemed to be in charge.

"Not allowed this side. Black bands only – expensive section. Yours is red band – cheap side."

Charming, love. Kick us while we're down, but it seemed about right. Everything about our tour was done on the cheap side, right down to the minivan, the lack of free water and now the second-rate lunch.

So we crossed over the invisible line that separated the rich from the poor and sat down with our gruel, hungrily eyeing the caviar and lobster across the way.

At 2.30 p.m., we finally arrived at Chichen Itza, seven and a half hours after setting off from the hotel. Unlike the ruins of Tikal or Copan, Chichen Itza was not set amid steamy jungles, but was in the middle of what seemed a tourist town, well-oiled to cater for the hordes passing through. By the entrance was a series of restaurants, bars and electronic barrier systems. With 1.4 million people passing through Chichen Itza annually (almost three times the number that Guatemala's Tikal gets and fourteen times the number Honduras' Copan ruins gets), it needed the barriers.

The Spanish contingent had already gone through, but we were told to wait. The reason was we needed an English-speaking guide but none were available. So to save time, the Chichen Itza authorities were lumping us with other sets of Brits who were arriving, so that, when a guide was found, we could all go off and see the sights together. Unfortunately, because we were all British, a moan-fest began. It appeared that everyone else had been mis-sold the Chichen Itza tour. One woman from Newcastle was the most vocal. "Eight hours to get here," she said. "Did we want to go to a pond in the ground? No, we didn't. Did we want to stop at a shitty souvenir stall? No we didn't. Did we want to eat in a crap restaurant? No we didn't."

"Which restaurant?" I interjected. "Was it the one on the square that looked like a transport café?"

"Aye. You were there, too, then?"

"Horrible food," Angela said. But then I noticed the woman's arm band. She was wearing a black one which meant that she had eaten in the posh right-hand section. And she still thought the food was terrible. Imagine what she'd have though if she had been in the Pauper Left Side.

After five minutes of prime grumbling, which made everyone feel better, a guide appeared – a bandana-wearing gent in his forties with a permanent smile. We all set off after him, high in expectation, low in energy. And then the trail opened up into a huge expanse of ruins, with the central pyramid being the star attraction. And I had to admit that the thousand-year-old temple was the best Maya pyramid I had seen so far on my travels.

"This is the Temple of Kukulcan," said the guide. "It is a step pyramid dedicated to the Serpent God." We all gazed at the pyramid, a structure that, since 2006, no one has been allowed to climb due to a woman losing her footing and falling sixty feet to her death. "Please follow me and listen." With that, he led us closer to the great pyramid and began slowly clapping. It was not a round of applause for us managing to get to Chichen Itza and keeping our sanity intact, but a demonstration of the temple's acoustic properties. A fraction of a second after each clap, an echo returned. Other guides were clapping to their groups nearby and then, to cement our lesson, our guide made us all count back from ten, each number punctuated by a clap and an echo.

"The echo sounds just like the quetzal bird," the guide said. "They were sacred to the Maya; their feathers were prized like jewels." He clapped again and we all listened more carefully. To me, it sounded like a regular echo and nothing really like any bird. But acoustic engineers had scientifically compared the sound of the Chichen Itza echoes to the sound made by the quetzal bird and found they matched very closely. Whether this was by coincidence or some deep-seated architectural knowledge that the Maya builders possessed is unknown. But how uncanny it was, I thought, to have a sacred bird's call reproduced almost exactly by clapping in front of a temple.

As well as the Temple of Kukulcan, the Chichen Itza complex contained numerous columns, platforms and a ball court, similar to the one I had seen in Copan, Honduras. And then, after only thirty minutes, our guide told us the tour was over.

I glanced at Angela. *That's it?* I mouthed.

The guide then gave a protracted monologue about having to rely on tips so that he could continue working at the ruins. "Without them, I am working for free," he lamented.

Cheeky bastard, I mouthed, as Angela rooted in her purse. About half of our group was doing the same, with the rest slinking off guiltily towards the souvenir stands trying not to be noticed. The guide was watching us closely but everyone was hesitating. How much should we give? What was fair? What would he regard as paltry? No one wanted to make the first move because everyone would see either how much of a skinflint they were or how generous with their money they were.

Sensing this indecision with his practised eyes, the guide told us how much a good tip should be. "Most people give two hundred pesos."

Almost immediately everyone began to pull out more cash from their purses, wallets or pockets, handing the bounty over to the man, who took it with bows and murmurs of thanks. As we all dispersed, Angela asked how much 200 pesos was worth; when I told her it was about eight quid, she looked shocked. Then she worked out how much money the guide had been given in total, a figure I'd already worked out.

She said, "So that means he received about seventy pounds for thirty minutes work?"

I nodded. "I know. He's onto a winner doing these tours. Say he gets five tours a day; he's making three hundred and fifty quid for less than three hours work. That's seventeen hundred a week! Seven thousand a month!"

We both looked at each other. That couldn't be right, could it? Seven thousand pounds a month? Surely not – especially when the average salary in Mexico was less than a thousand. But we had to wonder, especially with the guide already heading back towards the entrance where, no doubt, another group awaited him.

We walked towards the exit.

At 4.45 p.m. we all assembled by the old mini-van. With two hours to go before we got back to Playa del Carmen, I suggested to Angela that we get a taxi back to the hotel in order to avoid the hotel drop off.

"But we might be dropped off first on the way back," Angela pointed out. "Besides, how much will a taxi cost?"

"I don't know. I'll find out."

I went over to a couple of taxi drivers smoking under a tree near their cars. The price back to our hotel in Playa del Carmen, they told me, was a fixed rate of two hundred US dollars.

"Two hundred?"

"That is the price, amigo."

I turned around and walked back to Angela, accepting our fate on the merry-go-round of misery called the tour bus. When the driver turned up (fifteen minutes late) he told us there was one more stop on the way back. I sighed. Another stop after all this. It was almost too much to bear.

Angela gripped my hand. "One more stop and then we'll be back at the hotel. You can have a beer and relax, and then we can go back to that Mexican restaurant we were in last night."

An hour later, we arrived in the town of Vallodolid. And it turned out to be the best stop of all. Instead of gaudy tourist stores and overpriced cafés, Vallodolid was a little slice of authentic Mexican town life and, for once, I was happy to have a look around.

Vallodolid became a Spanish settlement in 1543, named after what was then the capital of Spain. The European settlers built their new town over the ruins of an existing Maya city, constructing mansions, churches, town houses and pretty plazas which looked great, but caused deep resentment within the local Maya population. Things reached boiling point in the 1840s when the Maya had a riot, killing scores of Europeans in the process. More locals joined in with the uprising and, with the Spanish heavily outnumbered, the Maya chased them away. Not much has happened in Vallodolid since then, apart from the town becoming a regular stopping point on Chichen Itza tours.

Angela and I emerged, blinking, into the evening sunlight bathing the town. While the Spanish contingent headed towards a burrito stand, we stood admiring the central plaza, an attractive area of fountains, statues and food stands overlooked by a tall church at one end. Locals sat around on the benches, happily chatting away; around the periphery were fetching restaurants and little boutique shops selling art and craft. One shop had a buxom skeleton dressed in a flowery frock, but we bypassed it on our way to a little restaurant just off the square called Loncheria El Amigo Casiano. The tortillas were cheap and cheerful but tasty as hell. The only thing spoiling the ambience was the presence of a local newspaper left on the table.

The paper was called *Por Esto!* which Google translated for me as meaning *For This!* Its tagline said the contents of it pages would be full of Dignity, Identity and Sovereignty. Well, I disagreed with that due to the front page.

Barbaric was the stark black headline. The photos offered no dignity to the people in them, because every person was dead, some without heads, most lying in pools of blood, all graphically shown in three horrible colour pictures. The story above the images described how masked men dressed as police officers had burst into a large marquee-type tent in the city of Tizayuca, central Mexico. At the time, the tent had been hosting a birthday party arranged by a person with connections to organised crime. After forcing their way in, the bogus officers pulled out machetes and decapitated seven women and four men in a reprisal, the article stated, for an earlier wrongdoing. I translated the caption beneath the grisly photographs. It read: Teenage hitmen ate their victims.

We pushed the newspaper away and finished our ground beef and tortillas in a sombre mood.

Angela was wrong about us being dropped off first. We were the last two people to arrive at our hotel. It was dark and it was pouring down and, when I looked at my watch, I saw it was 8.30 p.m., meaning our six-hour trip had morphed into a 13½ monster tour cooked up in the pits of Hell's furnaces. Because of the rain and the time, we could not be bothered going out again and so finished the day in one of the hotel's outlandishly expensive restaurants. No seats were available inside but there was a covered decking area outside which suited our purposes.

The outside patio also suited the purposes of a swarm of mosquitoes. While Angela sipped on her $13 margarita, a mosquito landed on me, though I never saw it. All I felt was the maddening itch after it had departed, closely followed by another itch just along from it. Both were on my sandaled foot, the favoured hovering ground of the flimsy blood-sucking insects. "Mosquitoes," I warned my wife who immediately put her drink down and swished her arms, looking beneath the tablecloth.

And then I felt something else. An almost imperceptible prick of almost-nothing pain. "Angela, is there a mosquito on my forehead?"

She looked up and her eyes widened. "Yes!"

I rushed up to grab at the minuscule vampire but it was already gone, shrilly buzzing past my ear. Then another landed on my arm and then one on my wrist. Angela had one on her arm, too and we both began swishing at them like people possessed. We got a couple, their fragile frames easy to swat into submission, and then Angela was plucking at one flying around her head, snapping her hands and then inspecting the catch. It was there all right, a blood-bloated female (as all biting mosquitoes are) squashed and red. My wife looked horrified and so did I. "That was probably our blood," Angela remarked but I was again distracted by a needle jab at my temple, and then at my ear. All around us, people were flapping their arms or else, like us, retreating inside. By the time we had returned to the sanctuary of our room, I was covered in seventeen bites and Angela in eleven. It was a fitting end to what had been, for the most part, a terrible day. We spent it scratching and itching until our bodies gave up and allowed us to sleep.

9

Two days later, on the long flight over the Atlantic Ocean to Manchester, the bites were still itching, and whenever I touched one, I felt the infuriating need to scratch it. I just hoped that the mosquitoes had not been carrying malaria, yellow fever, zika or dengue fever. But at least it hadn't been a swarm of kissing bugs that had attacked us.

Despite the end of the trip, I had really enjoyed my brief excursion into some of the countries of Central America and beyond. And when Angela asked me which country was my favourite, I had no hesitation in saying El Salvador.

El Salvador had surprised me. I had expected it to be a country down-at-heel, ravaged by rampant gang crime, with a capital city full of deprivation and pickpockets. And yet it wasn't, at least in the parts I had seen. It was the same with Honduras. When planning my trip to Central America, I'd purposely omitted Honduras from my itinerary, deeming it too dangerous to even consider. It was only in the final weeks, as I looked at my trip in detail again, that I considered Honduras. And what a good job I had, otherwise I would have missed out my second-favourite country.

I'd enjoyed Guatemala, too. Unlike Mexico or Costa Rica, Guatemala still had a frontier feel to it, a country at the edge where anything could happen and often did. Montego Bay, another hotbed of crime had been a worry, too, as had Belize City. But both had been wonderful places to visit. And that was the great thing about travel. So-called dangerous places could prove to be safe, worthwhile and downright exciting. Whether it was an equatorial capital in Africa or a gangland crime centre such as San Salvador, if a person played by the rules (i.e. did not venture into the danger zones, did not wear expensive jewellery and kept travel after dark to a minimum), things usually turned out okay. Most people in these places, I had discovered, were happy for visitors to see them selling fruit and vegetables in their roadside markets, to gaze at their colonial pasts and to glimpse tiny snapshots of their lives.

I sat back in my seat, trying to zone out the noise from the cabin as we hurtled through the night sky of the mid-Atlantic. And as I drifted off to an uneasy sleep, I thought of mountains, volcanoes and some of the friendliest people in the world.

CANCUN/PLAYA DEL CARMON
Top: The beaches of Mexico's Yucatan Peninsula are truly stunning; Angela
and me at Chichen Itza
Middle: Me wearing a Mexican wrestling mask; Skulls for sale are all over
Mexico
Bottom: Playa del Carmen Cathedral – the interior is well worth a visit;
Cozumel Island, just across from Playa del Carmon

Message from Jason

Thanks for reading about my travels around Central America. If you enjoyed it, I would really appreciate a review on Amazon. Just a few lines will do. Small-time authors such as me rely on word of mouth exposure. Just go to Amazon, type in the name of the book and leave a quick review.

If you have enjoyed this book by Jason Smart, then perhaps you will also like his other books, which are all available from Amazon.

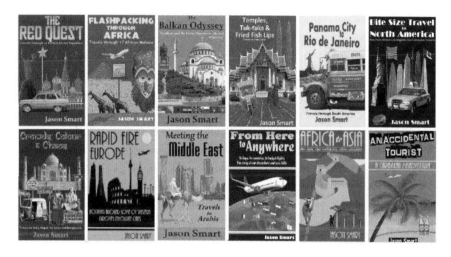

The Red Quest

Flashpacking through Africa

The Balkan Odyssey

Temples, Tuk-tuks and Fried Fish Lips

Panama City to Rio de Janeiro

Bite Size Travel in North America

Crowds, Colour, Chaos

Rapid Fire Europe

Meeting the Middle East

From Here to Anywhere

Africa to Asia

An Accidental Tourist

Hola, Amigo!

Take Your Wings and Fly

Visit his website **www.theredquest.com** for more details.

Printed in Germany
by Amazon Distribution
GmbH, Leipzig